FOR Susan —

Friends on the
journey of amazing
grace

Ray S Anderson

Judas and Jesus

Amazing Grace for the Wounded Soul

Judas and Jesus

Amazing Grace for the Wounded Soul

Ray S. Anderson

Cascade Books
A division of *Wipf & Stock Publishers*
199 West 8th Avenue, Suite 3 • Eugene OR 97401

Cascade Books
A division of Wipf & Stock Publishers
199 West 8th Avenue, Suite 3
Eugene, OR 97401

Judas and Jesus
Amazing Grace for the Wounded Soul
Copyright©2005 by Ray S. Anderson
ISBN: 1-59244-870-4
Publication Date: January 2005

10   9   8   7   6   5   4   3   2   1

We are born broken.

We live by mending.

The grace of God is the glue.

(Eugene O'Neil)

Contents

Preface

It was printed in block letters with a felt tip pen across the top of the mirror in the men's restroom in a restaurant in San Francisco: **JUDAS COME HOME--ALL IS FORGIVEN!** I stood quietly, watching as several men came and went, some glancing at the carefully lettered graffiti, but then passing quickly on. I speculated on the source. Was it some young man who had become a prodigal, having run away from home, now in desperation, trying to assure himself that his father might say these words to his own son who had become a Judas? Or, was it some father searching for a son who had betrayed and fled into the city, hoping against hope that he might read these cryptic words and dare to believe that even betrayal can be forgiven?

Following the publication of *The Gospel According to Judas* (1991, 1994), many have urged me to write a sequel delving more deeply into the dynamics of God's grace, which underlies both a theology of forgiveness and a process of healing and recovery for those who feel wounded in spirit and soul. While this book retains its original focus on the encounter between Judas and Jesus as a prologue, each chapter carries forward the theme of grace related to our own spiritual journey.

The story of Judas is the story of each one of us, to some degree. The past cannot be corrected nor failures erased by remorse. I suspect that the wounds to the soul of Judas were more deep and devastating than ours, particularly because they were largely self-inflicted. We all have such wounds, and one person's wounds are as painful as another's. It hurts to have failed others and even more than to have failed ourselves. When I reflect upon the story of Judas I feel a strange kinship with the kind of soul-sorrow that plunged him into the abyss of remorse and despair. These pains are the twinges of hell, which sear the soul like a raw nerve, stinging with fire at every step.

This is why forgiveness can be a superficial salve that does not penetrate to the depths of the pain. Are there wounds beyond the power of forgiveness to heal? Judas is the voice within us that will not be put to rest with platitudes nor silenced with sensible palliatives for nonsensical pain. Every step toward healing of that pain is painful. Is this why we recoil from even the touch of love and try to evade the grasp of grace?

Surely the divine lover is the relentless 'hound of heaven,' from which even Judas cannot escape. Where human love, even self love, turns away with regret, or even disgust, divine love persists and prevails as the amazing grace of God. It is of this grace that I write—of Judas and of the healing of the deep wounds to his soul. The healing begins for him as it does for us, with a meeting, a mending, and a mirror, in which we see ourselves reflected in the face of God.

Prologue

The Scenario

We dare not tell the story of Judas without recalling the story of Jesus, and of his tragic death on a cross and a glorious resurrection on the third day. There is a sense in which the resurrection of Jesus Christ from the dead jarred the logical sequence of past, present, and future out of sync. Matthew tells us that at the crucifixion of Jesus, "the tombs also were opened and many bodies of the saints who had fallen asleep were raised, and coming out of their tombs after his resurrection they went into the holy city and appeared to many" (27:52-53). The resurrection of Jesus created a time-warp, as it were, with death temporarily removed as the dividing line between those who live on both sides of this great gulf.

It is in this spirit that a conversation between Judas and the risen Christ might have occurred. As a literary device and an exercise in reflection on the depths of the grace of God, I have ventured into this warp in time occasioned by the resurrection of Jesus to create the dialogue between Jesus and Judas that we were never permitted to hear. Come with me to the place.

The Morning After

The confrontation between Jesus and Judas occurs in the very
place where Judas chose to take his own life. The cold wind
of death is stilled; the howling horrors of hell silenced. Satan
is held at bay. The power of darkness retreats in the presence
of the glorious light and life of the risen Lord. The relentless
logic of despair within the mind of Judas is made foolish by the
sudden appearance of Jesus in the lonely place to which Judas
retreated for his own final act upon this earth.

Judas is stunned, but not speechless. The skin on his neck
is bruised from the rasping pull of the rope which jerked his
head to the side. His throat is raw and hoarse from the shrieks
of despair he threw out into the night as he plunged into the
darkness. He involuntarily jerks his arm away from the touch
of Jesus. He will not be comforted. With a choking sensation he
feels anger welling up, its urgency giving way to words. . .

The Encounter

Why have you come to torment me? Aren't you
satisfied that I perished from this earth by my own
hands? Leave me alone, Jesus of Nazareth, let me go
to the hell I deserve. I betrayed you and delivered you
over to your own death. I said I was sorry, but sorry
isn't enough. Sorrow doesn't change anything.

*You are right, Judas Iscariot. There are things that do
not change. Though I am not the one who causes torment.*

Yes, that's true. I brought the torment on myself and on you, by failing to trust you and causing your death. Yet, I am tormented by your presence. You will probably tell me that you still love me, and so gain virtue for yourself and add another millstone around my neck. Don't you realize that for the betrayer love is a cruel reminder of failure? Go away! I have enough pain without your love punishing me further.

I come to say that you love me, and that is the cause of your pain and torment.

You're talking nonsense. If I loved you I would not have betrayed you. After all, betrayal is not an act of love, it's an act of treachery. You can't deny the logic of that.

Judas, betrayal is the sin of love against love. Unlike other sins, betrayal uses love to destroy what is loved. This is why betrayal does not end a relationship, why you cannot put an end to our relationship by yourself. Forgiveness for the act of betrayal seems impossible if betrayal is the final act. Yet betrayal is not the end of love. You hate yourself because you love me. You betrayed me because you love me.

For me, betrayal was a single, final, and fatal act; an aberration in myself for which I can find no cause. I expected you to speak of your love for me, but not of mine for you. What you're saying makes no sense to me. I can never know love again.

How can you stand there and say that I love you? How could this love be the cause of my torment and the source of my betrayal? You chose me--I didn't choose you. You called me to be your disciple!

In that you are correct. Judas, I chose you because you were given to me by my Father in heaven.

Oh, so I really had no choice! It was all a divine plan, and I was one of the pawns on your Father's game board! I resent that implication. For my part, I sensed an opportunity to fulfill my desire to serve God through the bringing in of his Kingdom.

Such strong desire to serve God has been called love.

Don't twist my words. Jesus, I became your disciple because I thought we had the same goal--to recover our land from the Romans and establish God's Kingdom of righteousness and holiness. After your baptism I heard you speak openly of the coming of the Kingdom. Many of us heard the same words from you.

I came not only with words, but the Spirit of God was upon me, performing signs and wonders of healing the sick and feeding the hungry. Were you not drawn to me along with the others by the power of my Father who loves the world?

You say drawn, I say seduced--by a power I didn't quite understand. And that sealed my destiny here on earth. Except for you I'd have been living a quite ordinary life, with my fanatical zeal partially tamed by unsuccessful ventures of political resistance. My friends and I would be sharing our dreams and telling our stories. But when you called me to be a disciple, I risked everything on that--and failed.

I understand failure. The other disciples failed as well-- they were scattered like sheep without a shepherd. I was left alone. You had each other, even in your failure.

Do you know that I went to them after betraying you and begged their forgiveness? They said that the devil had entered into me. They blamed me for everything. When I became your disciple, I began a friendship that turned out to be fatal for both of us. How can anyone call that love?

Tell me, Jesus of Nazareth--how did you decide to call me as one of the twelve? You say you chose me because your Father in heaven gave me to you. But why we twelve out of the many? Why me?

There was a decision to be made. I turned to the Father in prayer for guidance.

Are you telling me that I, Judas Iscariot, the man who betrayed you, am an answer to prayer? Do you still believe in prayer?

I did not pray so that every decision might be to my

advantage, but so that I might love every decision as affirmed by the Father who loves me. You are indeed an answer to my prayer; that is why I loved you and washed your feet on the very night that you betrayed me.

You knew even then, did you not, that I was plotting to betray you? Why didn't you stop me, or at least expose me as a traitor?

I knew, but I sought your love for me by sharing my love for you. I have prayed for you, Judas, that your love might return and that you might be healed.

I once prayed too. But no answers came. If I cannot love and cannot pray, what hope is there?

I'm confused. You tell me that I'm an answer to prayer and that you've prayed for me to be healed. But I sealed my fate with my fatal act of betrayal. Death was the final act of mercy that delivered my soul from the torment of life. I feel nothing, neither love nor hope.

How is it, Judas, that you feel such anger at me if you have killed all feeling?

Because you bring back to me all that I died to get away from. I closed the door to my life and sealed it with my own death. But now you've opened that door again. You have awakened all of the old feelings, but none that are new.

God is not the God of the dead, Judas, but of the living. Because I live, you also shall live.

Yes, I remember that you taught us that. But that had reference to Abraham, Isaac, and Jacob, who all died in faith. They may each have had many failures, but none of them failed as I did. My failure was fatal. I killed faith and tore the star of hope out of the black night, leaving only a gaping wound that will never heal.

And I have come to you through that tear in the fabric of despair, to touch your life again with healing grace and divine love.

But surely there are limits, even to God's grace! And I, of all persons, have passed beyond that limit. My name will be remembered without pity. My act of betrayal is my epitaph. No one weeps for me.

You were angry at me, Judas, for reminding you of your failure. Now you're bitter because no one weeps for you.

It is too painful to hear. You speak of healing and hope as though there were still time. But time has come to an end for me. One act of betrayal, like a drop of blood, has spread through the clear water that was my life, contaminating all. I poured it out on the ground. Never again can it be recovered--and if it could, it would be tainted with the blood of betrayal.

You feel sadness for what might have been, and despair over the irretrievable loss of your life.

Yes, of course! I loved my life and found joy in being your disciple. I really only came alive when you called me to follow you. But I see now that I ran ahead of you and tried to force you into following me!

I have had that temptation myself with respect to my Father. It is not easy to follow when your own desires are not those of your master.

But you did remain faithful, even when others denied you. In the end, you gained your life. In the end, I lost mine. Does not life teach us that what counts is how we die, not how we live ?

What counts, Judas, is not our foolish choices, but my Father's gracious calling. My choosing of you counts more than your betrayal of me.

I tried to deny the feelings of love I have for you. That's why my betrayal of you hurts so much. But our relationship can never be the same again.

We can never return to our innocence. The love that has suffered loss is a wounded love; it can be healed and made a stronger love.

You speak as though we have only had a lover's quarrel! I went beyond denial and even unfaithfulness. I burned the bridge that made our relationship possible. I cut the cord that bound my heart to yours and my hand to heaven. There is no way back.

That is true. There never was a way back. There is only a way forward. The past can only be returned to us out of the future. Love is greater than faith and hope, because it can heal faithlessness and cure hopelessness.

In a way that I don't understand, you place my act of betrayal and even death by my own hand between us as something that can be forgiven. You have awakened in me the memory of love, but not yet the possibility of its renewal.

To know that you did love me is sufficient to understand that I still love you.

But we have not spoken of the consequence of my action upon your life. My betrayal placed you on the cross just as surely as if I had driven in the nails with my own hands. Not even love can alter the fact that I caused your death.

My destiny was to do the will of the Father, and I was obedient--even to the point of death upon the cross. Your betrayal did not put me there. You can't take away from me what is truly mine!

I will always be remembered as the one who betrayed you. I had no explanation to give, no justification for my action. I regretted it immediately--but regret is a bitter tonic that never cures.

Betrayal is a transaction between two, the betrayer and the betrayed, with both having a certain power in the exchange. Your power, Judas, was to destroy the relation; mine to preserve it.

I tried to deny my love for you and became blind to your love for me. I have felt the power of that love, now that it is too late. If the sun could have stood still, and the hours and minutes slowed to an imperceptible crawl, there might have been time.

Do you think that all that is needed to redeem oneself is more time?

I speak only of enough time for you to have found me before I took vengeance upon myself by taking my own life. If betrayal is a transaction between two, death is a solitary act. And death by one's own hand is the most solitary of all deaths.

And you think that by taking your own life you sealed your fate and plunged into the realm that God has forsaken? I have been to the God-forsaken place, Judas; it was on the cross, not in the black hole in your own soul. One death in a God-forsaken way is enough; I have died that death--and behold I am alive!

I thought I could see , but I was blind. Through your eyes I see my life is no longer flat and one-dimensional. The door that I closed has become transparent. I--I see a different Judas on the other side!

It is not enough to use my eyes, Judas. I have touched yours so that you may see yourself, and for yourself, that you are my friend.

I saw my guilt, but not the shame that blinded me and angered me. I confessed my sin of betrayal and threw the money back at their feet. But something in me cowered like a child caught stealing coins from the box for the poor.

You have discovered what many have yet to see, Judas, that each failure is not merely an offense against God, but a loss of dignity and esteem for the self. Long before you met me, you wove a veil of shame to shield your eyes from the sight of that emaciated child.

Even in my betrayal of you, I sought to protect myself from exposure through a too-quick confession, as though I could merely undo a wrong. But I could not keep the shame from burning through and tormenting me to death. In the end, I crept within it and killed the child that could not be healed.

You are that child, Judas, and of such is the Kingdom of God!

1

Encountering Grace When We Least Expect It

The person speaking on my voice mail apologized for intruding, as though an act so fragile that it could be erased with the press of a button at my convenience was itself an offense needing forgiveness in advance.

"I think I may be beyond help. My life is an utter failure. I have destroyed my marriage; I am a slave to sins so wretched that I can only hate myself as much as God must despise me."

There was a long pause. Then slowly, each word placed with the deliberation with which one would deal a deck of cards when playing solitaire, he added, "I'm not sure why I called. You don't know me. I read something that you had written about Judas. I think I am Judas. You don't have to call back. . . . but if you should, my number is--------."

I did call. And even as I write this, we have begun a correspondence in which he pours forth his personal shame and spiritual guilt over an addiction that torments him like a defiant demon over which he has no control.

It is not strange to me that he identifies so strongly with Judas. From behind prison walls and in pastors' studies I have heard similar voices. They speak of Judas when they speak of what they have come to believe is unforgivable in their own life.

This why I write of Judas. Judas is a synonym for the unknown and unforgiving darkness that lies like a stone within us, resistant to the hammer of guilt and to the solvent of remorse. Like a "stony stalagmite," writes Anne Morrow Lindbergh:

> Mounting within the unconscious caves of night.
> No solvent left but love. Whose love? My own?
> And is one asked to love the harsh unknown?
> I am no Francis who could kiss the lip
> Of alien leper. Caught within the grip
> Of world un-faith, I cannot even pray,
> And must I love? Is there no other way?
> Suffering without name or tongue or face,
> Blindly I crush you in my dark embrace!

Judas was tormented by the unknown quality in his own life. He was overcome by the darkness, which he had concealed even from himself in his fanatical zeal to bring in the Kingdom of God by his own efforts. In a sense, he was too strong in his own efforts and, therefore, too brittle to bend when tortured by his own inner demon of remorse.

From his vantage point on the cross, perhaps Jesus could peer over into the very place where the body of Judas lay, having "bought a field with his blood," as Luke tells us in recounting his terrible manner of death (Acts 1:18-19). Bound by the soldiers, nailed to the cross, Jesus could not move toward Judas in order to intercept his senseless act of self destruction. Helpless, Jesus watched as Judas drowned in his own sorrow. No time for an opportunity on this side of death to remind Judas that grace and forgiveness cannot be lost by our efforts, because these are never promised on condition of our faithfulness.

Not in this life would Judas hear the words from the cross, "Father forgive." Never in his self-torment would Judas have a vision of the face of Jesus turned toward him with compassion and love. He sealed his destiny upon earth with a self-imposed verdict on his life, and surrendered himself to the community of those who were closest to him on earth for their final testimony.

In the sanctuary of his own personal pain and sorrow, Judas enacted the final ritual that would forever make him a public spectacle and offense to love. No sympathy was found for him. No eulogy spoken over his life. No remembrance that he had once been an answer to prayer.

MUST FAILURE ALWAYS BE FATAL?

Judas was a failure when viewed from the perspective of loyalty to Jesus and the other disciples. It is not that the other disciples kept their faith longer than did Judas and continued to be followers after Judas failed. Their following of Jesus came to an end on the same night "in which he was betrayed!" When Jesus was arrested and brought to trial, all of the disciples drew back. Peter's impulsive attempt to defend Jesus with the sword was circumvented by Jesus himself. Frustrated, Peter followed from a distance and, when questioned in the courtyard, denied that he even knew Jesus. Though John was present in the vicinity of the cross, along with the mother of Jesus, no other disciple is mentioned. Even after his death, none of the eleven disciples attended to his body. The two 'secret disciples,' Joseph of Arimathea and Nicodemus, arranged to have his body buried. No, the faith of each faltered at the end. But in the case of Judas, the final act of betrayal outweighed that of flagging faith.

When actions are contrary to the commitment of faith, as were the actions of all the disciples, we begin to make excuses, looking for human weakness in order to preserve an element of faith. We can make allowances for human weakness in living out our faith while still holding to the possibility of faith. We can excuse Peter as being weak in faith when he denied Jesus due to the circumstances in the final hours leading to Jesus' arrest. We can all identify with such weakness of faith. Nonetheless, along with Paul, we hope that through weakness the grace of God will be made manifest in our lives (2 Cor. 11:30).

When one elected to highest political office in the land becomes the object of a scandal involving sexual relations with a woman not his wife, we are told that the citizens on 'main street' are not interested in his personal weaknesses, even if they be called sins. "He is only human, after all," is the refrain. "Surely we can forgive his failures in one area of his life in light of his success in other areas."

Others raise shrill voices in protest. "He has betrayed public trust, and is no longer worthy to hold office." If, indeed, failure is linked to betrayal, it may well be considered fatal in the eyes of some. When this happens, one becomes a Judas.

With betrayal there appears to be no excuse, and so it is taken to be a sign that one is bereft of grace. Behind the name Judas lies the need to demonize the one who betrays. This is the failure that will often be judged to be fatal.

The biblical language is precise and unambiguous at this point with regard to Judas--then "Satan entered into him" (John 13:27). John drives the point home when he records Jesus calling Judas the "one destined to be lost" or, as some translate the phrase, "son of perdition" (17:12). We forget that Jesus used such language with others. Once he said of certain Pharisees, "You are of your father the devil" (John 8:44). On another occasion he said to Peter, "Get behind me, Satan! You are a hindrance to me; for you are not on the side of God, but of men" (Matt. 16:23). Surely Jesus did not intend to label Peter forever as a Satan! The restoration of Peter following the resurrection of Jesus is the act of grace and forgiveness that overcomes failure.

Jesus offers forgiveness for that which humans deem unforgivable. The act of betrayal on the part of Judas was a failure on many counts. It was a failure of his commitment to follow Jesus, even though that seemed to be leading to a failure of Jesus' own mission as the disciples understood it. Judas failed the other disciples also, by exposing them as accomplices in his willingness to point out Jesus to his enemies. But even after Judas had left the group to execute his act of betrayal, an act which was not hidden to Jesus, Jesus surely included him in his priestly prayer as one of "those whom you gave me out of the world" (John 17:6). Is there forgiveness for the unforgivable act of betrayal? Does failure have to be fatal? Does no one weep for Judas?

Upon entering Jerusalem for what Jesus knew would be the last time, he wept over it, records Luke (19:41). These were not only tears of sympathy for the suffering that would eventually fall upon the residents of that city for their hardness of heart, but tears of compassion for the very ones who would soon nail him to the cross. He had come to give grace not judgment, salvation not condemnation. "Father forgive them, for they know not what they do."

In his final hour, the failure of Judas shrinks to insignificance alongside of the terror of the cross for Jesus. When Judas viewed his own failure and the betrayal of Jesus as fatal, he made the mistake common to many. We tend to magnify failure, in others as well as in ourselves, because we so often look at the effects of sin rather than at the wonder of grace. Failing to live out of the freedom and security of grace, we fear Judas more than we shrink from the cross. For Judas is one of us, and if he can fall, so might we.

By his own action, Judas fell back into a world without grace.

He found no sympathy from those who paid him to betray Jesus and no forgiveness in his own heart. He embraced the darkness in his soul, not with love, but with unrelenting remorse and unrelieved guilt.

With Judas, we find no testimony to forgiveness and no place of atonement. Does the cross then lose meaning with regard to his failure? In the end, by his own estimation, Judas fell from grace, not having the assurance that the one who had chosen him held the power to extend grace to him. Judas forgot, or could not believe, that he was an answer to prayer. He tore himself out of the prayer life of Jesus and hurled himself to his own destruction, seeking in his desperation to make atonement for his act of betrayal. But Judas could not cast himself out of the gracious love of God, which first sought him out and called him to be a disciple.

Whereas humans reach a limit in what can be forgiven, there appears to be no limit for divine forgiveness. Is that really true?

CAN EVERYTHING BE FORGIVEN?

Simon Wiesenthal tells of an incident that took place while he was in a Polish concentration camp. A nurse took him to the bed of a dying SS Nazi, 22 years old. The solder, whose name was Karl, said he had to speak to a Jew, to confess his crime of murdering innocent women and children. He begged Wiesenthal, as a Jew, to forgive him so that he could die in peace. Wiesenthal said, "I stood up and looked in his direction, at his folded hands. At last I made up my mind and without a word I left the room." The German went to God unforgiven by man. Later, a fellow prisoner wrote, "You would have had no right to forgive him in the name of people who had not authorized you to do so. What people have done to you, yourself, you can, if you like, forgive and forget. That is your affair. But it would have been a terrible sin to burden your conscience with other people's suffering."

Human forgiveness has its limits. The man went to God "unforgiven by man." But our question has to do with God's forgiveness. The real question has to do with mercy rather than forgiveness. Is there a limit to God's mercy? Hardly, for if that were true, we would have to say that at the core of God's being there is justice without mercy. And that would be to contradict not only the actions of God, but also his own statements about his character as a merciful God. "Because the Lord your God is a merciful God, he will neither abandon you nor destroy you . . ." (Deuteronomy 4:31).

If forgiveness is not always a possibility, mercy is. There are people who may be beyond forgiveness on human terms, but, even as evil humans, they are not to be excluded from mercy. For in becoming merciless, we also become inhuman.

In showing mercy, one seeks to alleviate pain, temper justice, and restore relationships. While mercy is prompted by compassion, it has its source in the moral virtue of promoting the value of a human life when it least deserves it or cannot bear it. We applaud acts of mercy because we recognize the moral goodness of such actions, which go beyond the demands of the law.

While some people show no mercy because they have no compassion, others who have deep feelings of compassion are reluctant to extend mercy in fear of undermining justice. For some, punishment for violation of either a natural, civil, or divine law, is itself the moral content of the law. To release one from the consequences of breaking the law is considered by such people to be a violation of the moral law.

The moral value of mercy, on the other hand, is grounded

in the moral being of God and of humans created in the divine image. Forgiveness has to do with release from punishment, not exemption from the law. Mercy is shown to those who have no power or right to establish their own righteousness and human well-being. Mercy is a moral demand, while forgiveness is not. We cannot hold persons accountable to forgive when they have been sinned against, but we can expect them to show mercy where it is appropriate. Where forgiveness is offered, mercy has preceded it and constitutes the moral basis for forgiving.

In 1993, Amy Biehl, a 26-year-old Fulbright Scholar, was murdered by four blacks in South Africa while attempting to end apartheid by registering voters for the nation's first free election. Her murderers were apprehended and imprisoned. Her parents, Peter and Linda Biehl, went to Cape Town to establish a foundation in their daughter's name aimed at violence prevention, and they have continued to maintain a presence there as a continuation of Amy's commitment to peace. Under the newly formed Truth and Reconciliation Commission established to grant amnesty for political crimes to those persons who confess and give the whole truth about their actions, the four men who murdered Amy were given full pardon and release from prison on July 29,1998.

Commenting on this action, which they supported, Amy's parents said, "It is this vision of forgiveness and reconciliation that we have honored." They believed that this is what their daughter would have wanted. Peter Biehl then added, "We're not dispensing forgiveness. We're not God. But we support the decision." Releasing the men from further punishment in no way mitigated their crime, to which they confessed. Forgiveness in the form of amnesty, however, was an act of mercy that the Biehls saw as an important step in the journey toward peace and reconciliation.

The problem with Judas, as I am often reminded, is that he sealed his own fate when he took his life by his own hand. Those who hold this view argue that forgiveness is only a possibility this side of death, where there is room for repentance, and that death by one's own hand is a sin that allows no space for repentance.

After betraying Jesus, Judas found no grace in this life, and no opportunity for forgiveness, though he acknowledged his wrong and suffered bitter remorse. Now, when he least expected it, the very one whom he betrayed has approached him with talk of love rather than condemnation. This is an encounter with grace, but Judas is not prepared and strikes back in self defense against such a frontal attack of love. Deep wounds to the soul are exposed like an unhealed abscess, too painful to touch.

"Call me Judas," said the one who approached me through the anonymity and security of my voice mail. In his own eyes, he had fallen from grace, was bereft of hope and consumed by self-hatred. How does one speak of love to such souls? How does one receive grace when the soul is sick unto death and the core of the self is shattered? How can we receive grace when we are convinced that we do not deserve it?

2

Receiving Grace When We Least Deserve It

"Do you think Judas will be in heaven?"

The man who asked me that question sat manacled to the table in Los Angeles County Jail, sentenced to life without parole for the brutal killing of his mother and father. He carried in his hands an underlined copy of a book I had written about Judas, which had been given him by one of the volunteer chaplains.

"Can Judas really be forgiven for what he did? I did something worse than Judas, but somehow I believe that if there is hope for him, there may be hope for me."

We talked for an hour. He wondered how Jesus could ever forgive Judas, and whether what he himself had done might be unforgivable, even by God. He pursued the question to the point where I finally said, "Let me ask you a question. Suppose that when you die God confronts you with your parents whom you murdered and tells them that they now have the power to make a determination as to your eternal destiny. These are the parents whom you murdered. What will they say?"

He paused for a long while and finally said slowly, "My

mother will forgive me, for she loved me, I am sure of that."
To which I replied, "Then you know that God can forgive you,
for he is the source of love."

"Did you love her," I asked?

"Yes, but that doesn't make much sense does it? If I loved
her how could I have betrayed that love by taking her life?"

"What you are saying makes no sense," Judas told Jesus.
Indeed it doesn't when we think of love as our only security
from betrayal.

How can one both betray and love the same person? The
secret taping of one friend by another, as apparently happened
in a highly publicized incident involving a scandal surrounding
the president of the United States, caused outrage among many
people. "How could she do this to a friend? What kind of friend
would do such a thing to another?"

It was precisely the fact that a friendship was assumed to
exist that made the betrayal so outrageous. The outrage at the
secret taping was intensified because it was done to a friend,
not a complete stranger.

A stranger may expose a secret concerning me or break a
business contract made in good faith, but this is not the kind
of betrayal that strikes at the very heart of love and trust. Only
someone who has gained my trust can betray that trust. Love is
the ultimate act of trust between persons and carries with it the
seeds of betrayal. We can find reasons to explain the actions of
strangers, if not also a motive for excusing them. But betrayal
of love defiles sacred trust, defies explanation, demands retribu-
tion, and is the most difficult sin to forgive.

Betrayal is felt to be an unforgivable act because it exposes
ambivalence at the deepest core of human relationships. When
we cannot trust our own trust, and we dare not be loyal to
loyalty, we feel the cords that bind our deepest and most pre-

cious moments together slip out of our grasp. I think that this is why, if a Devil did not exist, we would need to invent one. The defection of what once was good to become evil cries out for explanation. Neither God nor humankind can bear the burden of introducing evil into what we all want to believe is essentially good.

Why is it that, while betrayal is a singular act, it has the power to destroy all of one's life, both past and future? Why is betrayal such a devastating failure in one's life with the power to condemn the past and contaminate the future? Why, for some, as in the case of Judas, does suicide, tragically, become the only personal atonement for betrayal?

Someone or something needs to be blamed for sowing the seeds of betrayal in the sacred soil of love. Our ancient ancestors talked of evil spirits, demonic possession, or looked to cosmic constellations for explanations. Shakespeare looked closer to home when he wrote, "The fault, dear Brutus, is not in our stars, but in ourselves" (*Julius Caesar*, Act I Scene 2). But what do we look for and what do we find when we look within ourselves? Mental illness may account for an act of betrayal as a form of temporary derangement; but if betrayal is an act of insanity, the ultimate madness may be the act of love, which makes us vulnerable, both to being betrayed and to becoming the betrayer.

When we probe further into the inner logic of love and betrayal we see that, while it may begin as the act of an individual, its effect hits a deeper nerve that connects the ligaments of love to the larger body of human social being.

The act of the betrayer not only contains the power to destroy a relationship; betrayal tears at the very fabric of human society. The very concept of betrayal is grounded in a structure of community based on loyalty, trust, and commitment. A lie

is not betrayal until it destroys the bond of friendship. "What
has shaken me is not that you lied to me," Nietzsche once said,
"but that I no longer believe you now." It is not the act of deception that is betrayal, but its effect in destroying confidence
in the one who is deceived.

THE SEEDS OF BETRAYAL IN
THE SOIL OF LOVE

Only where love and friendship exist is there potential for
betrayal. Every venture of love has in it the possibility, if not
the seeds, of betrayal. This tragic dimension of human experience was formed at the very beginning by our first parents.
When confronted by God after eating the forbidden fruit, Adam
pointed a finger at Eve and said, "The woman whom you gave
to be with me, she gave me fruit from the tree, and I ate" (Gen.
3:12). This is the same woman of whom he had just said, "This
at last is bone of my bones and flesh of my flesh." Fearful for
his own life, Adam pointed her out to God as the instigator. She
is the traitor, according to Adam; he is only her victim! Let her
perish if necessary, but let him survive!

For her part, Eve takes refuge in the existence of the Devil.
"The serpent tricked me, and I ate" (3:13). Desperate to shift
the blame, she originated the phrase, "The Devil made me do
it!" When we fail to find an explanation for a disciple who
becomes a betrayer, we look for some source of evil outside of
ourselves. Unwilling to consider that a disciple could do such
a treacherous act, the disciples account for the act of Judas by
saying, "Satan entered into him" (John 13:27).

The Devil is always someone else, no matter how fearful we
are of our own demonic impulses. The sweetest gossip among
friends is always the story that hints at another person's sexual

improprieties. The momentary relief that comes when the focus is turned to the scandal in the other's life betrays our own need of a Judas. And when we become the Judas, we then have need of a Devil.

Because we carry within ourselves the terrible possibility of betrayal in every relationship where there is love and trust, we have little mercy toward those who act out this betrayal. The sin most difficult to forgive in others is the one with which we live and against which we struggle in our own hearts. This is especially the case when we have succeeded in denying those deep impulses of betrayal and no longer are in touch with the dark side of ourselves. What feels like righteous judgment in urging condemnation of others who have been caught in betrayal may in fact be a blind and desperate need to reinforce the denial of our own propensity toward the same problem. None can be so cruel and without mercy toward others as those who have no mercy toward their own evil. Focusing on the sin of another is an effective device to cover one's own awareness of evil.

The act of Judas, for whatever reason, appeared to be one of deception. Pretending to be loyal to Jesus, he agreed for a sum of money to point him out to those who had already made it known that it was their intention to kill him, if necessary. A hundred others probably could have done the same thing, given the opportunity, for Jesus was a familiar face to many. The disciples might not have bothered to remember another person's name! But to have one of their own to do this terrible deed struck at the very heart and soul of their bond with one another and with Jesus. The fragility of their own loyalty, as revealed at the last supper, made each of them a suspect in their own eyes.

Jesus did not appear to be surprised, for he knew that human love always has in it the seeds of betrayal. He did not regard Judas as someone to single out for rejection. Indeed, at the end,

Jesus showed love and tenderness to Judas in washing his feet, along with those of the eleven. Jesus understood the terrible dilemma in the heart of Judas and included him in the last supper for the sake of empowering him to overcome the struggle within himself. He perceived Judas' desperate need to follow the course of his own agenda, even to the point of betrayal, perhaps in order to force Jesus to assume a more military and political stance with regard to the Kingdom of God. In the end, Judas tore himself out of the inner circle of love. Jesus did not cast him out.

No, the devastating damage done by a single act of betrayal is not due to the act itself, but arises out of the very community that has been betrayed. Who writes the history of our own lives? Is it not recorded in the perceptions and memories of others and written by the way that others choose to see us and remember us?

It is the very bond of trust and commitment which becomes the destructive agent in the act of betrayal, even as it is the constructive agent in redemption and reconciliation. The destructive power unleashed in betrayal is matched only by the greater power of love to heal through forgiveness. Even as Adam experienced the power of love and relationship through his commitment to Eve and her bonding with him, so he could destroy it by making of her disobedience to the divine command an act of betrayal of that bond. She is now his Judas. Her single act is construed by him to be the destruction of all that they had experienced as "one flesh." So powerful did this story become in the tradition that even the Apostle Paul remembers it from Adam's perspective. "Adam was not deceived, but the woman was deceived and became a transgressor" (1 Tim. 2:14).

Why is it so hard for Judas to receive the words of Jesus as a source of healing and hope? Why does Judas perceive the gracious presence of Jesus as a torment rather than a blessing?

It is because of shame. Shame has an insatiable appetite for self-abuse. What is offered as grace is devoured by shame and turns one sour and surly. Only when we understand the devastating shame that results from betrayal can we fathom the depth to which grace must go in order to produce healing and hope.

THE DEADLY POWER OF SHAME IN BETRAYAL

The power of the community in which betrayal takes place is enormous in the life of the betrayer. As I have said, the community creates the history of our lives for either good or bad. This is how we learn to perceive ourselves, as constantly under the watchful power of those who constitute our family and community. The self deeply internalizes feelings of shame and carries the familiar burden of wrongdoing. This internal sense of shame goes far beyond the guilt incurred for any single violation. Shame is a loss of our place with others and so is felt as loss of being. For our being is dependent upon how others view us. Those who have the power to create our history have the power to make us feel worthy or unworthy at the core of our being. More than guilt, it is the deep sense of shame, with its sense of loss of personal being, that drives many to suicide.

Tom was a successful attorney who was exposed as having embezzled money from a trust fund for which he was legally responsible. When his fraud was exposed, he took his own life rather than face his family and friends. At first he was willing to plead guilty and suffer the consequences, but his feelings of shame could not be so easily purged. Feeling that he had lost his place in the community of family and friends, he was driven to end his life rather than live with unending shame.

His family and friends did not understand. While they were affected and embarrassed by his actions, they wanted to forgive him and see him restored. They could not grasp the depth of shame that destroyed his being, because they did not comprehend the power that shame has in human relationships.

If we say, "I don't understand," concerning the actions of another, it is because of inner resistance to the idea that one of our own could do such a terrible thing. What we are really saying is, "I am not prepared to understand." There were some close to Tom, contributing to his self-identity and personal being, who felt contaminated by exposure to shame as experienced in relationship to him.

When shame connects to our own internalized sense of failure, we become unable to serve in the community of reconciliation and healing. Thus the shame, growing in the soil of self-blame and pain, sent out its shoots to take root in the larger community of which Tom was a part. Even as he repented and made restitution for his wrong doing, those around him moved back to protect their own innocence and projected upon him the mantle of Judas.

Very little is made of the fact that Judas had deep remorse and repented of his action of betrayal. Matthew tells us that when Jesus was sentenced to death by the tribunal, Judas went to the persons who had hired him for his treacherous act and said, "I have sinned in betraying innocent blood." When they refused to listen to him and stop the process, he threw down the money that they had paid him and went out and hanged himself (Matt. 27:1-5). It is strange that this action counts for so very little among Christians who read Matthew's account today. The disciples do not seem to give Judas any credit for this remorse. He offered repentance for his sin, but that did not seem to take away their sense of shame. Shame-based people find it difficult to forgive. They seek to compensate for their sense of shame by punishing others.

WE ONLY BETRAY THOSE WHOM WE LOVE

The paradox in the structure of community is that the very bonds of love and commitment that serve to create and sustain our identities can also serve to destroy us. This reveals how fragile even the strongest bonds between persons here on earth can be. Because we are not 'pure in heart' and each one of us carries within us the possibility of betrayal, our love can turn treacherous when betrayed. Yet we have no other choice! We do need each other. "It is not good to be alone," God said of Adam before the creation of Eve (Gen. 2:18). Created in the divine image and likeness, we can only experience and express that divine likeness through the bond of social and community relatedness. Is the only protection from betrayal not to love? Never to trust? The only security against never becoming a Judas is never to become a disciple.

The reality of love grows where the intentions of the heart are focused and shared. These twelve men grew to love each other, beyond their private agendas and personal needs. But in that love are also found the source of betrayal and the seeds of treachery. We can do injury to a stranger, but this is not betrayal. The very concept of betrayal requires that there be something to betray. And in betrayal it is love that is both the source and the object. We betray when we feel that our own love is betrayed by the failure of others. We become treacherous when we test the vision of love and find it different from our own. We turn the passion of love into raging anger and brittle violence when that which we love seems to resist our demands.

How else do we explain the fact that domestic violence and
child abuse is treachery against the people that we have promised
to love? What could account for the fact that 'normal' people
abuse and seek to destroy those with whom they live, other than
the fact that before there was betrayal, there was love? Only
when trust is first formed through shared life can it be broken.
And only the sense of outrage, fueled by a primitive moral
instinct and carried out with the passion of love's despair, can
wreak the havoc and destruction in a family and among friends
that betrayal causes.

For this reason, one cannot deal with the one who has
betrayed as a mortal enemy. At the core of the psyche of the
betrayer is failed love, not an evil spirit. Betrayers do not only
need a forgiveness that issues from the love of another, but also
the recovery of a love within themselves that has gone awry.
This is why it is so difficult for those who have betrayed others to be received back into fellowship through repentance and
forgiveness. For betrayal has torn the flesh of fellowship and
friendship away, leaving only the skeleton of love's despair vis-
ible. This is too terrible to look upon and too revealing of the
fear that hides in our own love. Such fear is too much for us to
tolerate. We need a scapegoat to carry off our sins.

I suspect that this is how it was with Judas and the disciples.
The association of the words traitor and betrayer with the name
Judas came from those who remembered him as a trusted disciple, not from the curious crowd. For most, he was only an
incidental figure in the larger drama of a religious quarrel that
ended in a crucifixion. But the disciples could not forget and
so chose to remember him only as a betrayer. In writing of his
history with them during the three years that he was a follower
of Jesus, one of the twelve, they label him even then as "one
who was to betray him." Pilate, who delivered Jesus over to be

crucified, and the soldiers who nailed him to the cross are treated more kindly by the disciples than Judas. Their actions can be forgiven because they can be understood as part of their official duties. At worst, Pilate is viewed as a weak and cowardly political ruler. The soldiers may be brutal, but they are loyal to their oath of obedience to Caesar. But the act of betrayal by Judas is a failure of a different kind.

Only a son can become a prodigal son. And once having become a prodigal, the son in Jesus' parable determined that this would never happen again. He would return to his father and confess his sin, but then live as one of the hired servants (Luke 15). Servants cannot become prodigals. They do not belong to the family in the same way as sons and daughters. While servants do not usually inherit the family fortune and are not usually included in the 'family story,' neither do servants become the 'family Judas.' Thus the son came back willing to give up his right of sonship, willing to live as a simple servant. In the parable as Jesus told it, the father would have none of that.

In the mind of the father, the son would return and live as a son, not a servant. But why must he always carry the label 'prodigal,' even when the father has restored him? Is it only the elder brother in the story who sees to that? Or are we all like the elder brother? Do we also find it more difficult than the father to say, "come home, all is forgiven!"?

The Father's story of his son will carry a different theme! "This my son who was dead is now alive," said the Father. Here we have a hint of the power of God's grace to create a new story of our lives. We are not merely "sinners saved by grace," but "children of God." We have been "born anew to a living hope," wrote Peter (1 Peter 1:3). We are no longer strangers and sojourners, wrote Paul, but we are "fellow citizens with the saints and members of the household of God" (Eph. 2:19).

The power to give new life is the power to create a new sense of belonging and a new community that serves as the basis for our identity and well being. Through God's grace we are born into a community that has been healed of shame as well as freed from guilt.

The love that calls us into relationships of friendship, marriage, and even discipleship can be very dangerous. Once we have been loved and drawn into fellowship we have been empowered to love in return. It is this love that binds us to one another and to God, and it is with this love that we have the power to deceive and the opportunity to betray. At the time of his calling to be a disciple, Judas had high hopes of idealism. It was the springtime of his life. His perception of following Jesus seemed to him a road to victory and a horse for his chariot. Now, in the dead of winter, with his soul frozen in despair and remorse, he wished it might have been otherwise.

He once could pray with confidence, now he distrusts even prayer. What he has yet to discover is that, despite his act of betrayal, he is an answer to prayer.

3

Experiencing Grace When We Need It Most

The woman sitting in my office was distraught and angry. As she talked, I began to feel that she had good reason to be so upset. Her daughter had a history of drug related problems, had stolen her mother's credit card, withdrawn a large sum from the bank, and left home to live with two other teenagers and a man twice their age.

"I am heart-sick over this," she told me "and angry. Angry not only at her for what she has done to me but angry at God for not protecting her." I encouraged her to talk about her feelings toward God: "What has God done or failed to do in protecting your daughter?"

"This is my only child. My husband and I almost gave up trying to have children. I read in the Bible where Hannah, who was without a child, prayed to the Lord, and she received a child in answer to her prayer. His name was Samuel. I prayed that God would enable me to conceive, and that if I did I would give this child to God in the same way that Hannah did with her son, Samuel. When my daughter was born I knew that she was an answer to prayer."

I waited.

"I kept praying for her, especially when she began to get in trouble. I wonder now if it makes any difference to pray. I wonder if there really is a God, and if there is, why he doesn't put a shield of protection around those who belong to him."

I thought about Judas. He too was an answer to prayer. One of the most compelling and convincing elements in the life of Jesus was his life of prayer. Not only did he pray frequently and regularly, he prayed in a way that astonished his disciples so much that they exclaimed, "Lord, teach us to pray!" (Luke 11:1).

"Now during those days," wrote Luke, "he went out to the mountain to pray; and he spent the night in prayer to God. And when day came, he called his disciples and chose twelve of them, whom he also named apostles: . . . and Judas Iscariot, who became a traitor" (Luke 6:12-16). There it is, Judas is an answer to prayer! How do we explain that?

Through the prayers of Jesus the dead were raised, the blind received their sight, the ears of the deaf were opened, the demons were cast out, and the loaves and fish were multiplied. Through his prayers in Gethsemane he received the wisdom and courage to be faithful until death, even death upon a cross (John 12:27-28; Luke 22:39-46). He prayed specifically for Peter and told him as much. "Simon, Simon, listen! Satan demanded to sift all of you like wheat, but I have prayed for you that your own faith may not fail; . . . ." (Luke 22:31-32). Following the crucifixion of Jesus, where Peter's faith indeed did fail him, and after the resurrection, Jesus appeared to Peter to re-confirm him as a believer and an apostle; the prayer of Jesus for Peter was indeed answered as he became the preacher at Pentecost!

But what of Judas? After the resurrection the disciples remembered that Jesus had prayed for Peter, but not for Judas! Are we to assume that Jesus prayed for the impetuous and unreliable Peter, but not for the ambitious and crafty Judas? Was Jesus selective in his prayers, and did he pray only for those whom he felt were worthy or who had the possibility of restoration? Can we really believe that Jesus would wash the feet of Judas, share with him the bread and wine at the Last Supper, and not also pray for him? Who else could have told us that Jesus prayed for Peter except Peter himself? But who remained after Judas took his own life to tell us that Jesus also prayed for Judas? Judas cannot tell us that, for he is dead. And the disciples could not be expected to tell us that because they would not have been aware of it. Or if they were, they could hardly be expected to mention it in light of Judas' betrayal and suicide!

WHEN OUR PRAYERS FAIL

In no area of the Christian life is there more uncertainty, confusion, and even a sense of failure than in our life of prayer. Many of us were taught as children to pray. Later, prayer was urged upon us as a source of spiritual renewal and blessing, as well as a way to secure God's provisions for our physical and spiritual needs. We were reminded of the answers to prayer achieved by many of God's saints as a means of challenging us to a deeper and more sustained prayer life. And yet, we so seldom realize answers for our prayers.

Our children for whom we pray are not always healed of disease and spared the pain of grievous loss. Friends for whom we intercede with fervent prayer still suffer catastrophic illness and lingering, painful deaths. Yes, there are the occasional almost miraculous exceptions to which we cling with nervous faith and of which we speak in a too-shrill voice, as if to fill the void of heaven's silence too long endured. But earnestly inquire of us

concerning our confidence in prayer to feed the hungry, heal the
sick, salvage broken marriages, produce saving faith in loved
ones, and we confess more failure than success.

We are not amazed that the prayers of Jesus were heard and
answered by the Father on each occasion when he prayed for
others. Yet we have come to expect that our own prayers may
well seem to go unanswered, or perhaps unheard. We know that
we do not pray as we ought and that our prayers so often are
desperate and devoid of the inner certainty which comes from
an intimate communion with God, our heavenly Father.

But we are surprised when we see that the prayer of Jesus
when he chose the twelve to follow him resulted in the calling
of Judas, his own betrayer. And we are left to question the ef-
fectiveness of Jesus' prayer when Judas was allowed at the end
to follow through with his evil act.

What do we make of Judas as an answer to prayer?

Whatever the consequence of Judas's act, it cannot erase this
fact, his life is no longer his own, but belongs to the Father and
the Son. As an answer to prayer, Judas has been grasped by an
intentionality that cannot be shaken by his own act of betrayal.
Judas no longer belongs to the world, subject to the fate of all
that lies outside of God's grace and mercy. Judas no longer is
part of the 'history of death,' which overtakes all the descendants
of Adam as a consequence of sin. Yes, had he not taken his own
life, he would have died of one thing or another, as will all of
us. But once grasped by the power of God's grace and love, we
are no longer under the power of death, but have the promise
of life beyond death.

Judas was not only chosen as one representative of the twelve
tribes of Israel as the elect of God; he has now become a representative of every person who is the non-elect. Judas stands as
the disqualified one, the one who forfeited his special calling

and squandered his inheritance. Judas stands as the apostate Jew and the uncircumcised Gentile. Judas is the Father's answer to Jesus' prayer for all humanity descended from Adam and Eve who have fallen from grace.

As an answer to prayer, Judas stands for each one of us and tells us that every person has a place in the love of God, no matter what our destiny here on earth. The gracious and redemptive love of God through Jesus Christ is an investment in the possibility of human persons, not a wager on our perfectibility. The possibilities of divine love are grounded in the actuality of God's redemption of his own Son from the "curse of the law" and the fate of death. The possibility of human life sharing in the destiny of God's eternal life is because each person is actually a human person, created in the image of God and 'given' by God to Jesus Christ.

So it is with Judas. He had the possibility of becoming a traitor and actualized that possibility as his own story and destiny upon earth. But he had actually been given to Jesus "out of the world" and so was actually given a share in the life of the Son to the Father and the Father to the Son.

The word traitor has been written on the face of Judas by those who tell his story here on earth. Jesus sees Judas as an answer to prayer, and sees in his face the possibilities that belong to every human life. Because we tend to make God's grace conditional, we look for signs of disqualification on the face of people; and we read into their lives failure and rejection, because we think we know their destiny. "Charlie Brown, you are the world's worst failure," scolded Lucy. "In fact, you have failure written all over your face; it's there; I can see it--it's failure, written all over your face." Charlie Brown found his dog Snoopy, and said, "Just look at my face; don't write on it!"

We have no cause to write on the face of Judas. We have no

right to disqualify him ahead of time simply because we know
his destiny here on earth. Nor do we have the right to treat any
other human person in that way. If Judas is an answer to prayer,
so might be the one who betrays us. So might we ourselves be
when we betray our own deepest desires and ideals.

What do we see written on the face of others? Anger, apathy,
bitterness, unfaithfulness, hatred, loneliness--these are self- designed masks that often cause us to judge others and deny them
the grace of God. We think we see the destiny of others when
we discover their latest sin or experience them in predictable
patterns of behavior. The list of people I would not choose as a
follower of Jesus grows daily! And in the end, when I look in
the mirror, what I see written on my face seems to disqualify
myself. When I remember that Judas was an answer to prayer,
I continue to pray for others and not give up. I remember that
Jesus continues to pray for me, that my destiny is decided by his
love for me, and that his choosing of me is unconditional.

LOVE RISKS FAILURE

No love is free from the risk of failure, not even the love of
God. This is what we learn when we see Judas as an answer to
prayer. Having received Judas from the Father, Jesus loved him
from beginning to end. I know that human love fails in its desire
for the good and well being of others; I know that the love of
the most faithful parent fails in many cases when their children
go astray. I know that my love fails when persons whom I love
continue on a path of self-destruction and that the love of others
for me fails to produce in me what they desire and hope for.

We explain the failure of love to produce perfection in others as due to our own imperfect love. But what explanation is
there for the failure of Judas when loved by the perfect love of
Jesus? Who would question the quality of Jesus' love? Who

would dare to suggest that someone else might have been successful with Judas where Jesus failed? No, we must learn here that love risks failure in order to redeem. Unconditional grace means just that. Grace is shown and given, even where the risk of disobedience and failure is certain.

Judas represents that unknown and unpredictable factor in every person. He was actually a disciple by the gift of God, the choice of Jesus, and an answer to prayer. Yet he was also potentially a betrayer, *as were the other eleven!* Let us not forget that. All of the twelve were a risk with the potential of betrayal, as each suspected near the end.

Yet we stumble at the actual betrayal of Judas as if that represents a kind of failure that is inhuman, that can only be attributed to "Satan entering him." We have difficulty explaining the fact that Judas could do such a thing and become such a person when he was chosen after a night of prayer. But this again reveals our inability to grasp the fact that prayer is not a means of removing the unknown and unpredictable elements in life, but rather a way of including the unknown and unpredictable factors in the outworking of the grace of God in our lives. Having made his choice, not on the basis of ruling out what was a threat, but of receiving the twelve as from God himself, Jesus could love each of them with the same unconditional love that he received from the Father.

PRAYING FOR OUR OWN JUDAS

This reveals to us how our life of prayer is based on our understanding of love and grace. When we view God's grace as conditional upon our perfection and success in living by his commandments, we will tend to use prayer as a way of securing God's promises by meeting the right conditions. In this view of God, a failure to produce a result through prayer throws us back upon our own lack of faith or, even worse, some spiritual defect that lies unconfessed and sabotages God's work.

On the other hand, if we view God's providence and fore-knowledge as some kind of 'pre-written history,' then we will use prayer to gain access to that secret knowledge of God--to take a peek at the answers in the back of the book, if you please! Thus we would expect Jesus, after a night of prayer, to have dis-covered what God already knew--Judas would be the betrayer. In the same way, when we pray we expect to gain an advantage in determining ahead of time the will of God so that we do not fail in some venture, or go in the wrong direction and have to 'back-track' in order to get back into the will of God.

What we discover, instead, is that the will of God is grounded in his promise as to the outcome of our lives, not in a detailed plan that remains hidden in the mind of God. Prayer is thus access to the divine promise revealed through the inner rela-tion that the Son shares with the Father rather than an attempt to avoid the risk of failure. Through his life of prayer with the Father, Jesus could love unconditionally and freely the unknown elements in his disciples as well as the known qualities. In this way, even the actions of Judas as betrayer are included within the divine promise and purpose for Jesus. Prayer, for Jesus, was not for the purpose of excluding the sinful actions of others, but for including all persons, despite their failures, in his own life with the Father as the basis for redemption of sinners.

In his high priestly prayer, Jesus not only prays for his dis-ciples, "whom you gave me," but also for all who would come to believe in the Father through Jesus. "I ask not only on behalf of these, but also on behalf of those who will believe in me through their word, that they may all be one. As you, Father, are in me and I am in you, may they also be in us, so that the world may believe that you have sent me" (John 17:20-21). The disciples are but the inner core of a circle whose circumference is as extensive as all of humanity.

Let all who read the story of Judas pause and ponder this mystery. There is an aspect of Judas in each one of us, an unknown and impenetrable darkness that we fear so desperately that we dare not give it a name. When it appears in others, its name is always Judas, and we are secretly glad of its destruction. We find no room for this Judas in our prayers, unless we learn how to pray with Jesus, the one who received Judas as an answer to prayer.

When our love has been destroyed and our faith in prayer exhausted, as it was for Judas, then our only hope is in the love and faith of Jesus. He does not come because we have prayed rightly and loved perfectly; but he comes into our prayerless nights and loveless days to become, once again, God's answer and a focus for our faith.

Judas come home, all is forgiven! There is a dialogue that continues beyond our own fatal attraction to death as the last word. Hope lies on the other side of that door of despair and death. Prayer is the opening of that door.

4

Saving Grace: Beginning the Journey Toward Healing and Hope

Jerry was a middle child. His brother Howard, older by three years, excelled in sports, graduated from college with scholastic honors, and became a junior law partner in their father's firm. Tony, his younger brother, was a 'surprise' to the family, as the story was told. Born eight years after Jerry, he was the 'family mascot.' A happy-go-lucky child, he basked in the glow of being everybody's favorite.

Jerry grew up not sure of how he fit into this family system. He felt accepted, but not loved like his younger brother Tony nor admired like his older brother Howard. During the years that he lived at home while attending college, he became concerned about his parents. They argued constantly, and his father increasingly became distant and even abusive, especially when he was drinking. When he talked with Howard about this, he was told to mind his own business, that their parents were adults and could work out their own problems.

A family crisis occurred during Jerry's last year of college.

Jerry dropped out of school with only one semester left and joined a local disco club band, where he played the drums, continuing to live at home. His father was furious; but after making an initial scene, he retreated to his routine of surly silence and minimal family participation. Suddenly, Jerry's mother announced that she was leaving and filing for divorce, stating as her reason the intolerable situation at home, with Jerry and her husband in a 'cold war,' as she put it. Howard, the older brother, sought to intervene by calling a family council. During the ensuing discussion and arguments back and forth, Jerry's father confessed that he never felt that Jerry had what it took to make something of himself. This was a shock to Jerry, but an even greater shock when his brother Howard turned on him and accused him of being the cause of the problem, saying, "I felt all along that you did not really fit into our family--but I guess every family has its black sheep."

This scenario has been played out in countless families and in a variety of ways; only the names and the circumstances change. We now know that every family is a system of inter-relationships and dynamics, with each participant assuming a role that contributes to the overall family dynamic and stability. When its stability is threatened, the family system quickly seeks to recover its functional stability, usually at the expense of the most expendable member. In this case, Jerry became the family scapegoat because he exercised the freedom to do his own thing.

When the story of that family is told by its surviving members, Jerry's label as the 'black sheep' will undoubtedly be traced back to the very beginning. No longer will the good days of family love and friendship be remembered. He has become the family Judas.

THE STIGMA OF BEING THE BLACK SHEEP

In calling the twelve to become his disciples, Jesus created something like a family. He had told them that they should be prepared to forsake all other relationships for the sake of the Kingdom of God. And this they did. Living, eating, and traveling together for more than three years, they no doubt experienced closer bonding than any of them had known before. For all of their different temperaments and agendas, they were bound together in a family-like system. Their arguments over who was to be the greatest is witness to this fact! The betrayal of Jesus by Judas was a devastating blow to the other disciples. How could such an act of treachery have been done by one of them? Will they too need a scapegoat on which to project their own uncertainties as to Jesus' mission and their own survival?

Judas gained his reputation as a betrayer through the selective memory of his former friends and disciples. In telling his story they excised whatever good he had done, and tell us only of the bad. Even in identifying Judas as a fellow disciple, John found it necessary to remind his readers that he was Judas Iscariot, "the one who was about to betray him" (John 12:4). In Matthew's account of the choosing of the twelve, when the name of Judas Iscariot was mentioned, Matthew added the editorial comment, "the one who betrayed him" (Matt. 10:4). Midway through the ministry of Jesus, when all others began to leave him, but the twelve remained, John recalled that Jesus said, concerning Judas, "Did I not choose you, the twelve, and one of you is a devil?" And to this John added, "He was speaking of Judas son of Simon Iscariot, for he, though one of the twelve, was going to betray him" (John 6:70-71).

In retrospect, John remembered Judas as the one who protested the actions of the woman who anointed the feet of Jesus with the expensive alabaster ointment by saying, "Why was this perfume not sold . . . and the money given to the poor?" And then, to make sure that we see the evil motivation behind this action, John added, "He said this, not because he cared about the poor, but because he was a thief; he kept the common purse and he used to steal what was put into it" (John 12:3-6).

At the last supper with the twelve, John tells us that Jesus foretold the betrayal by saying, "one of you will betray me" (13:21), and that after Jesus gave the morsel of bread dipped in wine to Judas, "Satan entered into him. . . and he immediately went out. And it was night" (13:27, 30). But it is also made plain in John's account that none of the other disciples had an inkling of this and, in fact, were so distraught by the statement of Jesus that they asked, "Lord, who is it?" Matthew reveals the uncertainty in the heart of each even more clearly by telling us that the disciples "began to say to him one after another, 'Surely not I, Lord?'" (Matt. 26:22).

In recounting for us the priestly prayer of Jesus just before the actual betrayal by Judas, John tells us that Jesus, in his prayer, accounted for the disciples who had been given to him by the Father, by saying, "none of them is lost except the one destined to be lost" (17:12). One searches in vain for some glimpse of Judas as the disciples must have known him before his act of betrayal. Where is the bond of emotional closeness and evidence of shared life that must have developed during those three years? Even Peter, who denied knowing Jesus when challenged during those last frightful hours, is remembered as a faithful follower and friend despite his failures.

Were the disciples so sure of the kind of man that Judas was that they felt free to depict him as a traitor and alien to them during the three years of close association? What made them read back into those three years his final act of betrayal in such a way that this entire period of his life should be discredited? There seems to be little regret that a man who once had been a friend and fellow disciple of Jesus could come to such a tragic end.

Is it because we are so unsure of our own stability and integrity that we deny sympathy to those who fall, lest we too be viewed as susceptible to the same failure? Did the disciples feel it was necessary to disown him and to deny any bond between him and them in order to conceal their own lack of certainty during those days?

I have known people to accuse one who expresses sympathy toward a fallen member of being unreliable. Such a person immediately comes under suspicion! Rather than risk this, we betray the betrayer for the sake of our own integrity in the eyes of others. This is a betrayal of love for the sake of preserving our own innocence. In this sense, Jesus 'lost his innocence' when he refused to betray those of us who are betrayers. He was known as a 'friend of sinners,' and became 'guilty by association' in the eyes of the self-righteous.

EVERY GROUP NEEDS ITS OWN JUDAS

I suppose that every community *needs* a Judas! Unable to deal with our own tendencies toward betrayal, kept in the secret of our heart, we quickly identify the one who gets 'caught in the act' as *our* Judas. We look for a scapegoat when the community in which we trusted fails.

Every church needs its own Judas. Every group of pastors and priests needs its own Judas. And every family has its own way of identifying the one who will serve as the scapegoat to carry off the relational failures and dysfunction that plague the entire family system. We all need someone to draw off the demonic in us. We still need someone whom we can blame and on whom we can project our own fears and fantasies. How often have we heard a parent say, "that child will be the death of me!" Or, one marriage partner say of another, "I should have known from the day we were married that this person would destroy my life." Betrayal begins when love blames.

When we seem to fail as parents, it is instinctive to attribute to the child some intractable and incorrigible temperament. No longer do we perceive the child as having a history of belonging and part of the family bond. When rebellion occurs, this is viewed as betrayal of all the love that has gone into parenting. The child's history is now re-written and the story that constitutes the basis for identity is told as though failure is written into the very bones. When we fail in marriage, the years of shared love and mutual commitment are erased, and the other's failure, even infidelity, re-writes the marriage relationship. We married the wrong person. Or to paraphrase the words of Jesus as John tells the story, "Did not I choose you, and you were a devil!"

To be sure, Judas became a betrayer by agreeing to point out Jesus to his enemies for a price. The eleven disciples also felt betrayed as they had trusted Judas as a friend bound to them in the dangerous and costly venture of following Jesus. But betrayal can work both ways. Is there not a sense in which they too quickly brand Judas as a 'devil' and 'thief,' pointing him out now as the traitor, while their own ambivalence and doubt go undetected? Is there not an element of betrayal of him in their refusal to remember and accredit the contributions that he made to their lives and cause? In seeking to erase those three years and re-write the story of Judas from the perspective of his final act of betrayal, they are cutting out part of their own history.

In the surgical removal of another person as a cancer in our lives, we often cut out a good deal of healthy tissue. And in so doing, we are likely to tear out the root of love and trust itself.

Perhaps this is why it is so difficult to forgive the one who is our Judas and seek restoration and reconciliation. This may explain the selective memory of the disciples concerning their former friend and fellow disciple. By retroactively seeing him as a 'thief' and a 'devil,' they can purge their own lives and consign him to the perdition that they fear that they could well deserve. Even after the resurrection of Jesus and his own reconciliation through a personal encounter with the risen Lord, Peter finds it impossible to allow any mercy to be shown toward Judas. His action of betrayal, Peter now feels, was in fulfillment of Scripture. Finding support in the Old Testament, Peter assigns Judas to total abandonment and urges a replacement. "Let his homestead become desolate, and let there be no one to live in it; . . . Let another take his position of overseer" (Acts 1:16, 20; Ps. 60:25; 109:8).

THE SAVING GRACE OF LOVE

Relationships such as Judas had with Jesus and the other disciples did not begin out of motivations and intentions of love, at least not as they would have understood it. The key phrases in the beginning were 'follow me,' not 'love me.' At the same time, love grows where the intentions of the heart are focused and shared in a vision, in a mission, in a common life.

An unlikely crew, the disciples nonetheless became vulnerable to each other through their common failures as well as successes. When their very existence is threatened by the elements, such as in the boat on the stormy sea, they huddle together in mutual terror and brotherly care for one another. When they

are attacked by the religious authorities for their commitment
to Jesus, they are reassured by his strong defense of them and
warning to others not to "despise one of these little ones" (Matt.
18:10). The personalities of each, as well as their strengths
and weaknesses, are forged into a chain whose links are strong
enough to withstand the forces that seek to divide and destroy
them, both from within and without. James and John are nick-
named 'sons of thunder'; Peter is the 'rock,' and Matthew the
'tax collector.' So too, Judas must have exerted his own strong
personality and presence among the twelve. We know that he
had leadership and organizational gifts, as he was responsible
for keeping the common purse, which no doubt meant arranging
for provisions as well as paying for them.

And what of their attitude and inclination toward Jesus?
If love grows where the intention of the heart is focused and
shared, each must have felt the tug of affection and strong
bond that linked them to Jesus as their master, teacher, and
friend. Judas too was captured by the power of Jesus' person
as expressed in his outpouring of love and compassion for the
poor, the sick and crippled, and for those who were outcasts
in society. They were drawn into his own ministry to these
people, offering the miraculous loaves and fish to the hungry,
laying their hands as well on the sick and feeling health and
life restored. Judas was part of the ministry teams sent out to
preach, heal, and cast our demons. He too felt the power of the
Spirit of God flow through his body and bring health and life
to those tortured by demons and disease.

How would Jesus tell the story of Judas? Would it carry the
same story line as that told by the disciples? I doubt it. There is
this difference between human love, fragile and sometimes fatal,
and the love of God. With God's love there is no insecurity and
ambivalence. God's love has no seed of betrayal, as evidenced

by his faithfulness toward Israel in their disobedience. The love of Jesus has no element of betrayal, as evidenced by his faithfulness, even toward those disciples who fled, and the prayer to his Father for the soldiers who nailed him to the cross, "Father forgive them . . . . " Surely Judas is included!

The gospel story is not merely one of God's love for humankind demonstrated through the death of Jesus on the cross as atonement for sin. The gospel story is God's story of our lives as seen through his love and grace. None can write themselves out of God's story--not even Judas.

Is there saving grace even for Judas? Where God's love reaches out to those who have fallen from grace there is saving grace. "God so loved the world" is the gospel of grace (John 3:16). And to drive the point home, the Apostle Paul reminds us that Christ died for the "ungodly. . . while we were still sinners" (Romans 5:6, 8). By his own testimony, Paul received the saving grace of God as the "foremost" of sinners (1 Timothy 1:15-16).

Saving grace is the beginning of a journey toward healing and hope in the place where we least expect it and when we least deserve it. Judas has encountered that grace, but like Lazarus who was summoned out of the tomb by Jesus, Judas remains wrapped in the cloths which bound him in death. "Unbind him, and let him go," Jesus commanded (John 11:44). The journey has begun when one has encountered grace and left the tomb behind. There yet remains the unbinding; this too is a work of saving grace.

For Judas, the cords of love that once bound him to Jesus have been severed and he is now entangled in them, like a drowning man being pulled under the surface of the water by the very life lines that were meant to save him.

"My failure was fatal. I killed faith and tore the star of hope out of the black night, leaving only a gaping wound that will never heal."

Jesus responds: *And I have come to you through that tear in the fabric of despair, to touch your life again with healing grace and divine love.*

Why is that so hard for Judas to hear and believe? Because he continues to be trapped in the relentless cycle of self-reproach. Until this cycle is broken, Judas will never feel the tender sweetness of mercy arising within his own soul. But there is still hope. Jesus still has work to do in the soul of Judas.

5

Empowering Grace: Ending the Cycle of Self-Reproach

"I've learned my lesson," the man said, sadly, as he began to pick up the pieces of a broken marriage. "I will never look at another woman as long as I live."

He was duly contrite. Caught in the act, he had no recourse but to confess and take responsibility for his actions. Consequence is often a more effective teacher than commandment. I knew, however, that the lesson that he had learned was "never get caught." And that what he really meant was, "I will never get caught with another woman again!"

His contrition was grounded in self-reproach. While self-reproach may be a good coach, it is also an unforgiving mentor.

Judas has learned one of the hard 'lessons of life.' He has learned that betrayal is an unforgivable act. A traitor no longer has a place within the community that gave him birth and a sense of belonging.

In our upside down world, we make our lies to be the truth and our failure to be the fact. The truth is, we insist, Peter did lie and Judas did betray; it is a fact. We cannot untell the lie, it

remains a truth that condemns, no matter how often we wish
in our minds that we did not speak it. We cannot change the
facts that tell the story of our betrayal. There are too many
witnesses, and our own hearts will condemn us, even if others
should forget. The lesson we learn is that it is our actions that
are the final verdict upon our lives.

This is why the suicide of Judas is such a stumbling block
to our minds if we should attempt to find some final hope for
his salvation. We treat promises as conditional and betrayal as
unconditional. Life is viewed as provisional and death as final
and fatal.

Even the promises we make and the commitments we un-
dertake become untrue when faced with the fact of betrayal.
The first words we speak don't count in the end. What counts
is loyalty to these words and faithfulness to the promises we
make. Our last words become the truth even as our last actions
become our epitaph. "But Judas Iscariot, one of his disciples
(he who was to betray him), said, . . ." (John 12:4). This is our
fate, is it not!

Do we not live in fear that some foolish act will become
our epitaph? Do we not carry within our own consciousness, if
not our conscience, labels that stick to our names? We have all
told lies that harden into truths and betrayals that have become
facts, that stick with an adhesive that no sorrow can dissolve.
The weight of these burdens diminishes self-integrity and in-
creases the magnitude of self-reproach.

There is no way that one can minimize the fact of the betrayal
of Jesus by Judas, nor is there any way to soften its effect. It is
a devastating and destructive act. The core of the self in Judas
does not shrivel to nothing through this loss to his very being.
Filled with despair, it balloons to grotesque proportions, obscur-
ing all else. The inner dialogue of self-reproach and remorse

blows shame out of proportion, filling the space once made complete with love for Jesus.

VIEWING LIFE FROM A DIFFERENT ANGLE

This is not how the Kingdom of God perceives reality! Jesus' teaching about the Kingdom of God turns upside down, or right side up (!) our view of reality.

"Blessed are the poor in spirit," said Jesus, "for theirs is the kingdom of heaven" (Matt. 5:3). "You know that the rulers of the Gentiles lord it over them, and their great ones are tyrants over them. It will not be so among you; but whoever wishes to be great among you must be your servant,. . . just as the Son of Man came not to be served but to serve, and to give his life a ransom for many" (Matthew 20:25-28).

In life, as Jesus knows, what really counts is not what we have gained or lost, whether it be fame and fortune or success or failure; what really counts is what we receive from the hand of God. Judas had been given to Jesus by the Father as an answer to prayer! Judas had been chosen and appointed as a disciple by Jesus. Everyone knows that betrayal of the trust given to Judas is an act of treachery and treason against that trust. Betrayal is measured by its effect; there can be no greater betrayal than the betrayal of the Son of God, for it is a betrayal of divine love and trust.

Viewed from the angle provided by Jesus, however, what really counts is not the betrayal of Judas, but the reality of a relationship constructed from the side of God. Judas did not choose to follow Jesus, he was chosen. This we must remember. While Judas may stand in our minds as the poster child for failure, in truth he stands beside Jesus as one placed there by God. This is the apparent paradox of faith. In the movement of our faith, which must motivate us to "take up the cross," we accept the reality of being chosen as the will of God that determines our destiny. While it is our faith that must accept the reality of being "children of God," it is not by our choice or will that we have this status (John 12:13).

What really counts is that our abiding in relation to God is upheld from God's unconditional love, not from our imperfect love. True, we make our choices and to some extent determine our own destiny on earth through those choices. But sooner or later we find the fabric of our faith grows thin; and when it tears, we can only attempt to patch it up with more promises--"I will never again!!"--or yield to the vicious cycle of self-reproach.

Without a deep assurance of the abiding reality of our choices for God based on our being chosen by him, we will have difficulty believing that there is a bond strong enough to hold others to us when we fail them. What we fear the most is that others will discover this fatal flaw in our own love and abandon us if we should fail. Driving this fear deep within, we enter into relationships and make promises with a desperation that is concealed sometimes in eroticism and at other times in fanaticism. The erotic need is the desperation to find satisfaction through being completed in another. The fanatical need is the desperation to find meaning for life by joining a cause that obliterates our fears as passion burns with pure and all-consuming fire.

If Judas was bound to Jesus by erotic attraction, it was that he saw Jesus' charisma as power that he could appropriate for himself. If Judas was drawn to Jesus by love, it was a precarious love, a fascination fueled by the elixir of power and the romance of adventure. Such love can become treacherous when the romance dies and the adventure palls. Judas' hidden fear of rejection and abandonment became an inner rage and began the calculations that led to betrayal.

If Judas was attracted to Jesus out of desperation to find one willing to challenge the political power of Rome, in the end, Jesus failed to match his own fanatical zeal. When desperation is the bond that joins one to another, it often leads to fanaticism. The 'cause' becomes the compelling reason for the relationship. With betrayal of the cause on the part of the other--Jesus clearly wanted no part of a revolt against Rome--Judas delivered Jesus to his enemies, partly in spite and partly with the covert hope that Jesus would be provoked into a reaction where once again they could join in common cause.

Judas began as a chosen disciple and served for three years as part of the inner circle around Jesus. In the end, he turned traitor and betrayed Jesus with a kiss.

My choosing of you counts more than your betrayal of me, Jesus tells Judas. It is as though Jesus said, "Your betrayal hurts, but my choosing heals. You unraveled the cord that I used to draw you to me, but you could not break it. You did not choose me, but I chose you, and appointed you to go and bear fruit, fruit that will last. . ." (John 15:16).

CAN BROKEN RELATIONSHIPS BE HEALED?

"We are born broken," wrote Eugene O'Neil, "We live by mending. The grace of God is the glue."

All betrayal is part of a dialogue and bond of relationship. It cannot be a solitary act, for in that case it would not be betrayal. For betrayal to occur, there must be more than one party involved. Thus, the person or persons betrayed are bound up in the action.

This is the difference between sin and sickness. What the Bible speaks of as sin is always a transgression of a relationship with God and with others. What society often calls wrong or inappropriate behavior, psychologists often trace back to emotional or mental illness.

If the failures and dysfunctional behaviors in our life are due primarily to some defect in our personal life, then we are offered a cure rather than forgiveness. On the other hand, if some of our actions are actions against the bond of love and trust by which we exist in relationship with God and others, then healing, not merely the overcoming of a defect through forgiveness and restoration, is necessary.

Peter denied the Lord through an untruth, and so sinned against the relation. One could account for Peter's denial as a defense mechanism by which he was instinctively acting to preserve an inner sense of security in the face of the threat to his life in that context. Because Peter's denial was overheard by Jesus, Jesus himself became the silent partner in a dialogue of denial where only Peter spoke. Consequently, Peter is forgiven and restored through the power of a dialogue with the risen Lord, where Peter now must speak words of love in response to Jesus' probing question, "Do you love me?" (John 21:15-19).

The point is this: we must view the actions of Judas in betraying Jesus as part of the dialogue between Judas and Jesus that began with the choosing of Judas by Jesus. Seen from this angle, the sin of betrayal is already contextualized by the greater fact of the relationship. Betrayal is the negative evidence that the relationship is real. For without the reality of the relationship, betrayal is not possible. The positive evidence of the relationship continues to exist as an actuality bound up in the personhood of the one betrayed.

Judas' betrayal of Jesus does not have the power to destroy the on-going dialogue of relation between Judas and Jesus based on the choosing. Jesus has the power to continue the relationship by means of love and forgiveness. This means that a continued dialogue is possible, based on the intention and power of Jesus as the betrayed to re-open the relation and so produce reconciliation and restoration.

The healing of broken relationships is always a possibility that issues from the power of love to embrace the wrong done to it for the sake of maintaining the relationship and restoring fellowship and love. Because betrayal is a sin against a relationship, the betrayal is evidence that the relationship is real and not an illusion. This challenges both parties in the relationship to discover its power to heal itself through the resource of divine love and grace poured into it.

For Jesus to say to Judas, "my choosing of you counts more than your betrayal of me," is to reiterate a profound truth. Jesus has expressed the same truth in other ways. He said it in many different ways as he entered into dialogue with the Jews, whom he called, "the lost sheep of the house of Israel" (Matt. 15:24). He made it the theme of the parable of the prodigal son and put it into the dialogue as the father demonstrates his love to the son at his return. "For this my son was dead, and is alive again; he was lost, and is found." He reassures the elder son, who wants to write the story of the younger son as a history of betrayal and label him with the epitaph "he has devoured your property with prostitutes." Again, we see sibling rivalry leading to the betrayal of the bond of family love. Yet, even with the elder son, the father creates a dialogue based on grace and gift: "Son, you are always with me, and all that is mine is yours" (Luke 15:11-32).

In the story, the prodigal son returns, not daring to be received as a son, only as a hired servant. So too, Judas concluded that his failure stripped him of his role as a chosen disciple and left him bereft of love and fallen from grace.

Is the sudden and tragic death of Judas by his own hand a just punishment for his sin of unbelief and evidence that he cannot be forgiven? Does Judas forfeit all that belonged to him as a follower and disciple of Jesus through that single act? If we think so, what comfort and hope will we have in our darkest moments, when unbelief, if not betrayal, comes down like an iron curtain between us and God? Does dialogue with God depend upon our faith or upon his coming to us in the darkness and solitude of even our unbelief? What was never verbalized between Judas and Jesus was written by John, "By this we shall know that we are of the truth, and reassure our hearts before him, whenever our hearts condemn us; for God is greater than our hearts, and he knows everything" (1 John 3:19-20).

The betrayal of Jesus by Judas was taken by others to be the final word by which the fate of Judas was sealed and by which the story of his life was written. But through God's grace we know that no sin can be the final word in our life, nor can death as the consequence of sin be the final word. Through the resurrection of Jesus, God destroyed the power of death to seal our fate. God's grace is the final word for all humanity. No death can overturn that word, even death that is self-inflicted. When God raised Jesus from the dead, the power of death to determine human destiny was forever destroyed. It is God who determines the destiny of even those who die unforgiven, as did Judas.

Judas, blinded by remorse and bludgeoned by self reproach, stumbled headlong into the abyss of his own despair. Renounced by his fellow disciples and bereft of family ties, he flailed with futile outrage against the dark forces that cast him like an orphan from the bosom of father Abraham—an abandoned child.

For all of the pain in remorse, it is ineffective and futile. Remorse always returns to the scene of the crime, wishing it might be different. But each visit only tears open the wound, and fresh blood pours out. For remorse, there seems to be an inexhaustible source from which to bleed new pain. Remorse, like grief, always keeps the wound open and seeks to keep the pain alive. As C. S. Lewis once put it when tracing the trail of grief back to the painful loss of his wife: "They say 'The Coward dies many times;' so does the beloved. Didn't the eagle find a fresh liver to tear in Prometheus every time it dined?"

Who will cover him with grace and connect with him in love? Where is there healing for the unhealed wounds of self-reproach and bitter remorse?

The words of Jesus haunt Judas as he sinks deeper into the darkest depths of soul sorrow. *You were angry at me, Judas, for reminding you of your failure. Now you're bitter because no one weeps for you.*

Is it merely self-pity that drives us to desire the care and concern of others when we no longer care for ourselves? Or is there something in us, like an embryo of hope unborn, that refuses to give up our grasp for grace even when we least deserve it? Thomas Wolfe, in his classic novel, *Look Homeward, Angel!,* called it the "great forgotten language, the lost land-end into heaven."

"Which of us has known his brother? Which of us has looked into his father's heart? Which of us has not remained forever prison-pent? Which of us is not forever a stranger and alone? . . . Remembering speechlessly we seek the great forgotten language, the lost lane-end into heaven, a stone, a leaf, an unfound door. Where? When?"

THE SPIRIT OF ADOPTION

At the core of our being, we are spiritual orphans seeking a way back home. The grace of God may be likened to the adoption of an orphan child. The apostle Paul, himself rescued from his own fanatical and fatal plunge into the abyss of a murderous rage against the Lord, writes, "We were by nature children of wrath, like everyone else. . . strangers to the covenants of promise, having no hope and without God in the world." But through the grace of God, he adds, we are "members of the household of God" (Ephesians 2:3, 14, 19). Through the grace of God we have received the "spirit of adoption. . . it is that very Spirit bearing witness with our spirit that we are children of God" (Romans 8:15, 16).

Through God's love we can become children of God through spiritual adoption. Our family and home are not our natural birthright, but a gift of grace. When we have lost our way, we can, through God's grace, find our way home again.

Into our extended family has come a child through adoption. As I reflected upon the significance of my grandson, who would someday come to realize that he has two mothers, one who chose to bring him into the world and another who chose to become his mother through adoption, I realized that this was a double blessing. Instead of perceiving that he was not wanted by his birth mother, he will come to understand that the desire to give birth and to place him with nurturing parents was also a choice of sacrificial love. As I prepared for the child's christening and baptism I wrote a poem, part of which reads:

Alive!

Torn from the perspiring flesh of others
we scream our pain with fresh-born fears
and reach out blindly for our mothers,
who bind us close with love-torn tears;
    a baptism into life.

Chosen!
Twice wanted means twice blest!
a first birth born with love's consent
to give you life and prepare what's best,
a gifted birth and second advent;
    a baptism into family.
      Christened!
In script invisible to all but grace
the water traces out your name;
I write God's image upon your face
and touch your soul with Spirit's flame;
    a baptism into Christ.

Why was it so important to me that something be said so that this child could have the assurance that he was desired, wanted, and that he was chosen? Is it because we assume that only adopted children may grow up with the fear that they were once not wanted?

In a deeper personal and existential sense, we are all adopted children! Subsequent to our biological birth, when the umbilical cord is severed, we experience another separation when our needs are not immediately met and the caregiver disappears for what must seem like 'forever' before returning to attend to us. What psychologists call 'separation anxiety' is only a technical phrase for 'abandoned to hell' as experienced by our infant psyche. We emerge gasping for air and immediately begin grasping for security as our world grows larger and we grow smaller. Our physical birth does not itself join us to the lives of others. We are all adopted children who had to learn our names from people who did not have to love us, but chose to do so.

There is in all of us a secret chasm that separates us from our bond of birth. It cannot be healed by looking back into our origins, but only in the love that comes to us out of our future. Some of us are precariously perched on the edge of this abyss, and some have slipped into it, like Judas. There are, it seems, failures that have opened up fissures in our lives too deep ever to be healed. There are betrayals that we fear have broken whatever bridges we had back to those who once loved and trusted us.

We have all experienced the bond of belonging. We knew the feeling. We believed the promises, danced at weddings, and cried for joy at a new baby's birth. We were secure in our feeling of always being 'at home.' But it can slip away from us so quietly that we do not realize that we have lost our connection. Or, suddenly we wake up to the fact that we have burned our bridges behind us, and we have no confidence in the future.

We know too much of Judas, because we know too much of our own desperate urgings and darkest fears. We are afraid when we are too close to the failure of any relationship. We often keep our distance because we fear that the same failure could happen to us. But there is also something compelling about Judas; and if there is perhaps a way back home for him, then perhaps there is for us as well.

6

Renewing Grace:
Awakening the Memory of Love

Judas recalled the feeling of anger when Jesus first said: *I tell you that you love me, and that is the cause of your pain and torment.*

The burning anger burst into flame when he responded, "Go away! I have enough pain without your love punishing me further." Now, in retrospect, he is grateful that Jesus continued the dialogue. But what do we do with gratitude when the house in which we live has been demolished and there are no walls on which to hang it?

The anger has now subsided. In its place is a feeling of confusion along with a sliver of hope, which he dare not acknowledge, lest it be the last flash of setting sun rather than a premonition of dawn. Encircled by the darkness of despair, he can no longer sense with certainty the difference between a rising and a falling.

The frightening thing about slipping into total despair is the loss of a sense of direction. It warns of the beginning of insan-

ity. Things can go terribly wrong in our life; but when the sun
no longer rises in the east, and the moon has disappeared into
the dark of the night, can we still speak of love?

AWAKENING THE MEMORY OF LOVE

As Judas pauses and ponders, he recalls the words of Jesus:

*Judas, betrayal is the sin of love against love. Unlike other
sins, betrayal uses love to destroy what is loved. This is why
betrayal does not end a relationship, why you cannot put an
end to our relationship by yourself. Forgiveness for the act
of betrayal seems impossible if betrayal is the final act. Yet
betrayal is not the end of love. You hate yourself because you
love me. You betrayed me because you love me.*

"You have awakened in me the memory of love," Judas now
confesses. Is that fair?

Memory has both a sweet and bitter taste when it touches the
sensitive palate of reflection. One of the marks of mental health
is the merciful gift of forgetfulness. If every hurt and every loss
were carried in the front of our memory bank, we would be in
constant pain and continual despair. Some people's memory
always is in the default setting, to use contemporary computer
terminology. Each time one awakens to the day, the memory
bank 'loads up' into consciousness the painful memories that
the night has suppressed.

What we desire is a memory that filters out pain and retains
pleasure. Sometimes this works too well when denial closes out
reality. For love does not cancel grief, but creates the capacity
to grieve through to grace, where memory itself is retained, but
healed of its power to condemn.

Jesus does not want to help Judas erase the memory of his

act of betrayal, but to discover in that betrayal the memory of love. For it is the memory of love, sometimes hidden within the deeper recesses of our failures, that becomes the source of our hope and healing.

Nor does Jesus wish to intensify the guilt of Judas, but to awaken in him the memory of love. For it is not guilt that empowers us to seek reconciliation and healing, but love.

Did Judas love Jesus? Certainly, but however that love was expressed, it was created by the love that Jesus had for all of his disciples. Did that love die somewhere along the road, so that Judas in the end acted out of absolute indifference or the passion of hate? I doubt it. For Judas was far from indifferent about the mission of Jesus, and destructive passion can often be traced back to love gone awry.

Judas mournfully exclaims, "I cut the cord that bound my heart to yours and my hand to heaven. There is no way back."

What Judas lost in his sin of betrayal was not his humanity, but the power to sustain faith, hope, and love as the core of his very self. In isolating himself, even from the community of others whose faith also faltered and who also lost hope, he was cast back upon himself and perished in his own self-remorse. When Jesus approaches Judas for the purpose of intervening into the vicious cycle of self-reproach, he must awaken in him positive motivations for self-love and self-worth.

Hopelessness, as well as faithlessness, is part of the sickness of the soul that results from the splitting of the self into positive and negative aspects that cannot be integrated into self-acceptance. Left with hopelessness, we cannot receive the love of others in such a way as to restore the battered self isolated by the effects of sin. Only the grace and love of God can restore health to the self whose worth can be affirmed by the love of others.

While there is no explicit command to "love oneself," it appears to be assumed as the basis for the motive power to love others. The command of Jesus to love one's neighbor is grounded in the assumed reality of "love of oneself" (Matt. 22:37-40; cf. Lev. 19:18).

This may sound heretical to those who insist that the human self is so desperately wicked and sinful that it must be expunged and replaced with a 'new self.' But the source of all love for God as well as for others is love of oneself. The source of all love for God comes from within the self, which is created in the image of God. Thus love of self is grounded in the divine image, not in the self as an object of love. Love of oneself is respect for the image of God in the self. This love is necessary for love of God and others.

Religion has tended to be more concerned with the eradication of sin and the implanting of a 'new nature' than with preserving the self. Psychology has tended to be more concerned with restoring the self than with providing a new nature through the empowering gift of the grace of God.

Many have found in psychotherapy some relief from the pain, if not a cure for hopelessness. If one can be relieved of guilt, one no longer seeks forgiveness. Is that really what we need?

Could Judas have been saved from his suicidal intentions and action through the intervention of a skilled therapist? Perhaps. But we would be deceived in thinking that this is the fundamental dilemma of Judas! For what Judas has lost is more than can be recovered through therapeutic adjustment and renewed self-esteem. Judas has lost a vital and essential relationship with God, and only the grace of God can restore that relationship.

Judas is not looking for emotional and mental survival skills in a world where the logic of sin and death casts its relentless spell over all of our hopes and aspirations. He is looking for "the lost lane-end into heaven," as Thomas Wolfe once put it. Judas longs to hear the words, "Come home--all is forgiven."

HOW TO REMEMBER THE PAST

Remembrance of the past often causes powerful feelings to rise up within us, not all of them positive. For example, I think about the time I made a miscalculation during navigator training for the Air Force and got hopelessly lost over the gulf of Mexico. The same feelings of embarrassment and humiliation at having to call the pilot and ask him to use the radio to get us safely back to base remain as powerful in my mind today as then, though the incident occurred over 50 years ago. Why is this so?

What keeps this incident alive in my personal past are my feelings, not the facts. I cannot recall the exact date, the name of the pilot, or anything else about the incident. It is the feeling that I have about myself that keeps the event from slipping out of my past, as have a myriad of other incidents.

The past is secured by feelings, not by facts alone. Feelings are always experienced in the present tense. What I think may be old feelings or emotional reactions that I experienced in the past are really present feelings that I have in relating myself to previous actions and incidents. It is the memory of the incident that triggers the present feelings. Certain feelings became associated with the memory of the incident and thus give the appearance of being past feelings. In reality there are no past feelings, only recollection of past events, which stirs up present feelings.

In our emotional dilemmas we make hundreds of new beginnings and a thousand promises to ourselves, as well as to others. But if these all are swept away by the undertow of our negative emotions flowing as cross currents in the sea of our past, we get caught up in a riptide of confusion.

Feelings are more about the self than about facts. The feelings that I had when I made a miscalculation and had to admit that I was lost were about being a failure. I had only myself to blame. Even worse, I was incapable of rectifying the mistake and felt utterly inadequate. These were negative feelings about myself. My self-esteem suffered a loss; I felt miserable and shamed. These are the feelings that fix this event in my personal past.

How do I know that I had these feelings at the time? Because recall of the incident stirs up some of the same feelings in me today. But I have other feelings about myself that are part of my present life. When my past follows me, I give it a present. I test out my feelings about being a failure because of a past incident by other feelings that I have about myself, which are positive and self-affirming.

It is true that we cannot rewrite history, but we can revise our own past. Because our past is secured by feelings, not by facts alone, we can revise our feelings about ourselves and thus about our past.

When I allow the memory of that incident to evoke feelings of complete failure, I find myself cramped into the narrow space of my navigator's cubicle, cut off from everyone else, and alone with my feelings of self-blame. When I do this, I allow the facts to take my feelings prisoner. My past then dominates my present.

But when I view the incident from the perspective of my present feelings about myself, the past is disarmed of its power to pull me back into that isolation chamber of failure and shame. When I have done that, I have revised my past by giving it a present.

As a result, the incident now can become an anecdote, a

story that I tell. Secure in the feelings that I have about myself as a person of value despite many inadequacies and failures, I have revised my past by viewing it through my present feelings about myself.

In my mind I wish Judas had not taken his life and had survived the vicious cycle of self-reproach. I wish that he had experienced healing and reconciliation with Jesus and the other apostles whom he also betrayed—being included again in the same kind of fellowship that they experienced with Jesus after his resurrection. I can then hear him telling the story of his betrayal of Jesus in somewhat the same way as the Apostle Paul later told of his actions against Jesus prior to his conversion (Acts 22:4-5). The betrayal of Jesus will always be a factual part of the biography of Judas. But he could have forgiven the past, because he found forgiveness and grace in the present.

HOW TO FORGIVE THE PAST

The association of confession with wrong doing is one of the oldest traditions of the Judeo-Christian tradition. The story of King David is one of the most celebrated and remembered events in the history of Israel. Desiring to have Bathsheba, the wife of another man, he took her for himself and arranged to have her husband murdered.

He covered up and denied the act. Eventually, however, Nathan the prophet confronted him and enabled him to confess: "Then I acknowledged my sin to you, and I did not hide my iniquity: I said, 'I will confess my transgressions to the Lord,' and you forgave the guilt of my sin" (Psalm 32:5). Nathan was also the one who heard this confession and gave him assurance of forgiveness: "Now the Lord has put away your sin; you shall not die" (2 Samuel 12:13).

There were indeed consequences of his actions; the child born to Bathsheba died. Confession is not a way of avoiding consequences, but of "restoring our souls," to use a somewhat quaint, but comforting biblical expression. "Do not take your Holy Spirit from me," was David's prayer. "Restore to me the joy of your salvation, and sustain in me a willing spirit" (Psalm 51:12).

Nathan was a person who evidently had the unusual quality of empowering another person in the moment of their greatest vulnerability and weakness. This is what is meant by unconditional love. It is a love that permits no deception, but offers healing and hope with no strings attached.

Dietrich Bonhoeffer, a German pastor who entered into a conspiracy against Hitler for the sake of the Jews who were being systematically tortured and exterminated, spoke often of the reality of human relationships as a context and criterion for the reality of divine love and forgiveness. Aware of the futility many people experience in attempting to find healing and restoration in their private appeals to God for forgiveness, he suggested that it is only in the context of the other person that we really find acceptance and healing.

"Our brother breaks the circle of self-deception. A man who confesses his sins in the presence of a brother knows that he is no longer alone with himself; he experiences the presence of God in the reality of the other person. . . . Mutual, brotherly confession is given to us by God in order that we may be sure of divine forgiveness."

Confession has to do with restoration, not regret. Confession has to do with renewal, not with ritualistic self-abuse. Confession is moving out of isolation into relationship, out of pain into wholeness and integrity.

Confession has to do with inner healing and the restoration

of self-acceptance and self-love. Self-love is not a feeling we can achieve on our own. Rather, it is the reflection within our own self of the unconditional love of others.

Confession is good for the soul, we are told. That is true, but it can become a trite saying and a means of cheap grace. What is good for the soul is the restoration and healing of our wounded spirits. Confession in the context of unconditional love is not a religious ritual but a human and personal encounter that bares our soul in pain and bathes it with the healing water of acceptance and affirmation.

In confession we break through to certainty of God's forgiveness, Bonhoeffer reminds us. Certainty delivers us from the anxious feelings that we have yet to be punished enough for our past. Certainty frees us from the compulsive need to manipulate others into giving us assurances to feed our deeply entrenched insecurities. In reaching certainty, we have cut the infinite distance between us and divine love down to an arm's length. Confession is not for the sake of erasing the past, but is a threshold of consecrating a new birth of hope.

HOW TO CONSECRATE A
NEW BIRTH OF HOPE

A second son was born to David by Bathsheba. David gave him the name Solomon. Nathan the prophet brought a message from God, indicating that this child was to be named Jedidiah--"beloved of the Lord." Therefore David gave him the additional name, which consecrated this new life with the divine promise of renewal of hope (2 Samuel 12:24-25). David too was consecrated with a new birth of hope, which he acknowledged in blessing the child and giving it a name signifying this new beginning.

For David, the intervention was one of divine grace, as I suspect all creative beginnings are. Having the consequence of his actions explained to him by the prophet, and accepting those consequences as facts, David no longer felt it necessary to continue his negative feelings about himself as merely a consequence of his sin.

Somewhere, in the life of each one of us, there exists that which God loves and blesses. Disguised as a friend, counselor, or a priest, a Nathan speaks the word of God concerning that which God loves in us. This stirs and attracts our feelings in a far deeper and richer way than the events and incidents in our past. This is what David discovered, and this is what led him to consecrate the gift of forgiveness and hope.

Judas has yet to make this move, however. He is still trapped in his pain and self pity, attempting to dissolve all consciousness in the solvent of bitter remorse. Judas reminds us that the journey toward healing and wholeness must pass through the most narrow passageway that a human can take--the solitary descent into the abyss of despair. The 'sickness unto death' for which there is no human remedy must yet be cured by the grace that transforms.

7

Transforming Grace: Envisioning Life in the Shadows of Death

I was once asked to officiate at the funeral service of a young mother who, on a bright and sunny spring day, dropped off her youngest daughter at her husband's place of work and inexplicably went home to take her own life. The family members were stunned and stricken with grief and remorse. "Why could we have not seen that she was suffering so much?" they asked. "Yes, she had some problems, but she seemed to be coping with them well enough."

I discovered that she was noted for her beautiful garden and her love for flowers. Lovely vases filled with fresh flowers could be found in every part of her home. At the grave side service, I commented on that, and said something like this: "Peggy herself appeared to be a beautiful vase. Yet, from the inside, she saw her life as cracked and falling to pieces if she let go of it. Nor could she hand it over to someone else to hold for her, for it took both hands to keep it together, and if she even took one hand off to ask for assistance, she feared it would fall apart. What we saw was a beautiful person, like a vase, with imperfections to be sure, but with no fatal flaws. What she saw from the inside were fractures that never could be mended. Her life broke from the inside out. Only in this tragic end do we feel her pain as a bond with her and with God. His grace is now her healing and our comfort."

WHEN THE DESIRE FOR LIFE IS LOST

We are living in days in which apparently healthy persons deliberately take their own lives rather than face the fears of an uncertain future. The increasing incidence of suicide among teenagers shocks us into the recognition that the insulation that protects our society from the terror of meaninglessness has become frayed and worn thin. Behind the shining faces of our children lie the skeletons of ancient fears for which our world of science and technology has no comfort. Beneath the surface of success flows the torrent of an untamed river that seeks to suck us into the vortex of future shock. It is as though we have no present, only the rapidly receding past and the onrushing future, which promises more isolated weariness and fragmented pleasure.

The desire for life, inherent at birth, is sustained by most of us, despite sometimes enormous discouragement and pain. For some, the thoughts of suicide are random whispers that lack substance, like images of a bad dream that disappear when exposed to the waking hours of daylight. For others, these become nagging voices begging consideration as the 'final solution' to daytime life, which has become a living nightmare.

This inborn desire for life can become weak under the layers of accumulated living where the burden of life becomes greater than its beauty. When thoughts of suicide become an insistent obsession, the desire for life must be repressed even further. One cannot entertain both notions, that of desiring to live and that of intending to die. The desire to live must be silenced in order to focus the self on the intention to die.

I have conducted graveside services for two persons who took their own life. I have talked with some who have tried and failed. I have talked with many who think about suicide; some seem to be obsessed with the idea. But no one has ever talked with one who actually took their own life--no one has come back to tell us what the final motivation was, what made the intention a final act. Even with Judas, one can only guess what drove him to this desperate and tragic conclusion.

One might call the suicidal impulse or obsession a sickness unto death, like a condition that attacks the immune system of one's vital life force. But it is a sickness of the soul, a twisted and distorted version of life that becomes a compelling vision of death. For those who attempt to prevent it, it appears as the ultimate insanity. For those who attempt it, I suspect that it becomes the only passageway of sanity in a world and life gone insane.

There may be, in the thought of suicide, a simplicity that seems to offer a light at the end of the tunnel, a way to transform life's vexations into a vision of escape. The logic of self-annihilation becomes inexorable, its wisdom brilliant, its outcome peace. It can be a powerful argument against the logic of living when the battleground is the psyche of the one immersed in despair. For each person's life has its own logic, and the reasonableness of another's is senseless to our own when we are pushed to extremity.

Judas has not slipped into total delusion. He takes responsibility for his actions. His mind operates with a clarity that offers no relief from the glare of self-accusation burning through to

the very core of his being. The relentless torment of self-in-
crimination becomes a tidal wave carrying him forward to the
unavoidable act of self-destruction. What, on other days, would
have been an intolerable thought now becomes a viable alterna-
tive. If he finds no forgiveness, neither from others nor from
within himself, then execution becomes a final act of justice of
the self against the self.

WHEN THE SELF BECOMES ITS
OWN EXECUTIONER

The tragic death of Judas by his own hand need not have
happened in the way that it did. He was caught in the logic of
sin, guilt, and death and saw his own death as the inevitable
consequence of his sin. One might even find support for such
despair by reading the biblical account of the human dilemma
as though divine judgment were the final word. But this would
be to miss the main theme of the biblical witness to God's grace,
where the final word is not judgment but mercy.

On one occasion, a disciple of Jesus inquired about a man
born blind from birth: "Rabbi, who sinned, this man or his
parents, that he was born blind?" (John 9:2). For the disciples,
this was a perfectly logical question! They no doubt had been
warned by their parents and instructed by the synagogue teachers
to avoid the consequences of sin by being careful not to violate
the law of God. "It is only the person who sins that shall die
. . ." (Ezekiel 18:4).

When this logic of cause and effect has been drummed into
the mind by teachers and used by parents to frighten a child
into performance acceptable enough to earn their praise, one
develops a conscience rooted in fear of condemnation. If one

could reason backwards from the evidence of God's judgment, to the sin that caused that judgment it might seem logical and simple as long as it happens to someone else!

Judas found himself in the position of having betrayed the very one who is the fulfillment of the law and the prophets. "I have sinned," he said, "I have betrayed innocent blood." And so he had! Having the psychological need to punish himself supported by the axiom that "the person that sins shall die," Judas followed the logic to its inexorable conclusion and took his own life.

I have no hesitation in saying that this is sick psychology and bad theology! There is a better psychology and a worthier theology when we view our lives from God's perspective. It was sin that produced the deep sense of shame which Adam and Eve felt and that led them to conceal themselves from the other and from God. The healing touch of God upon their lives removed that shame and restored their self-image even as it restored them to relationship with each other. It is the grace of God that transforms our inner life from self-disgust to self-worth. It is the love of God which empowers us to love ourselves in order that we might then love others.

From the very beginning, God intervened, and the terrible logic of sin and death was broken before it had a chance to claim its first victims. Adam and Eve both sinned, but they did not die. Instead, they were restored to life (out of death) through divine intervention. God pointed to the terrible consequence of sin when he warned, "in the day that you eat of it you shall die" (Gen 2:17). This death as separation from God goes beyond the physical death that is natural to all creatures, including the human, taken from the dust of the ground. Under the torment of this death as separation from God's life, the self suffers both psychologically and spiritually long before physical death occurs. The consequences are real and terrible in their power to destroy.

But our spiritual state is not determined by the consequences of sin but by the counsel of God. "I have no pleasure in the death of any one, says the Lord God; turn then, and live" (Ezekiel 18:32). God stands between us and the consequences of sin, with his law in one hand and forgiveness in the other. Perhaps the teachers of the law did not tell Judas that. He was led to believe that the law stood between him and God and that only through obedience to that law could he have hope of entering into God's Kingdom.

The self becomes its own prosecuting attorney and builds a file of evidence against which there is no defense. Justice, not mercy, is the demand of law. The self may seek mercy, but when the self is also the accuser, the trial is short and the judgment swift. When the dialogue stays within our own minds, sin quickly turns to sickness of soul, for which there is no forgiveness. Forgiveness requires some word from the other who is the one sinned against.

In the case of Judas his action of betrayal is not merely a defect or weakness of character. Instead, his act was directed against Jesus, and so Jesus became the silent partner to his own action. If Jesus remains silent and does not speak, if there is no word that comes to him from the other side of death, Judas is cast back upon himself in remorse, guilt, and shame.

For Judas now to defend his action, he must face Jesus, not someone else who is also under 'sentence of death,' but the living presence of Jesus who died, but whom God made alive. The dialogue is no longer within the mind of Judas, but between Judas and the one whom he betrayed and who now stands before him.

A dialogue between Peter and Jesus is recorded in the Bible

following the resurrection of Jesus. Jesus relentlessly asks Peter the question, "Do you love me?" Each time Peter is forced to confess that he does until, by the third time, he has erased the effect of the three times he denied Jesus when he was apprehended and sentenced to death (John 21:15-19). Peter received healing and hope and became a faithful follower and one of the founders of the first Christian community.

There is no story of a similar dialogue between Jesus and Judas after the resurrection, because Judas had taken his own life before Jesus was raised from the dead. From the story as we are told it, the chronology of betrayal, death, and resurrection is logically fixed, so that Judas forfeited his encounter with Christ by taking the prerogative of determining his own death. It is as though, in death, Judas has forever shut the door between himself and Jesus that even the resurrection cannot open.

In the resurrection story, however, we are told that Jesus appeared to his disciples "through closed doors" and moved in and out of their closed-in lives with perfect freedom according to his 'own time.' The event of resurrection, like the crucifixion, did occur within the world of time and space, subject to this world's chronology of past, present, and future. Time cannot be reversed, despite the popularity of such notions and our fascination with movies such as *Back to the Future*. But in the resurrection we are not dealing with only an historical event, which it surely was, but with a radical transformation of this world of time and space and its logic of life and death.

The story of Peter is one of failure, shame, remorse, and restoration. The story of Judas goes deeper than that. For Judas, failure became fatal. Not only did he hate himself for what he did, he killed himself out of that self-hatred. It requires no more than a little artistic imagination to re-create the despair of Judas—one need only to acknowledge the death-wish that

lies behind the moments of despair in each of our most hopeless moments. "Why did I not die at birth," cries out Job in his
distress. "Why is light given to one in misery, and life to the
bitter in soul?" (Job 3:11, 20).

One who feels like that knows well the sickness unto death.
This kind of sickness of the soul describes a broken spirit. The
question is, what is the cure?

HEALING A BROKEN SPIRIT

The metaphor of brokenness carries a variety of meanings.
Those who become casualties of abuse, failed marriages, chemi-
cal dependency, moral failure, or excessive grief are assumed
by many to be 'broken pieces' floating around the 'mainland'
of a functionally stable community. Or, to change the metaphor
to that of an ocean liner, broken people are like those who fall
overboard and are either left to drown or pulled back on ship as
a survivor. Even when one is 'recovered,' the stigma of being
a survivor seems to imply instability and, perhaps, diminished
trustworthiness.

We often refer to people who have gone through a crisis as
'broken people.' From the outside, it appears that a divorce
leaves one a broken person, or that one becomes broken down
with grief.

The healing process begins where the broken edge becomes
the growing edge. All brokenness brings emotional pain for
which there is no rational relief. The healing of emotional pain
is the spiritual work of the self. Growth does not come through
emotional change alone, but through the life of the spirit. It
is the spirit that expands the self and directs the self toward
growth. The feelings of the self are the core of subjectivity and
individuality. The spirit of the self constitutes the openness of

the self to the spirit of others and, essentially and ultimately, to the Spirit of God.

When I look into the eyes of those who have experienced the shame of being caught in a moral failure I do not often see hope. Even where forgiveness has been offered, restoration of hope does not always result. Forgiveness that does not lead to hope and the recovery of the joy of life is not good enough. The human spirit seeks the recovery of hope even though one is offered formal forgiveness. How can we find restoration and hope when we are flawed beings?

The circumstances that cause one to suffer pain and distress of soul may be quite different. For some, it comes as a result of their own actions; for others, from being a victim of abuse or the blind and senseless ravages of natural life. We can become broken in spirit through the abuse of others just as surely as through our own failure and foolishness. In a very remarkable way, however, the process of recovery and restoration is quite similar in each case.

And herein lies a profound truth.

The brokenness of the human spirit is a deeper and more creative edge than guilt and remorse for sin. A sense of guilt is not creative and produces no positive motivation toward spiritual wholeness. We tend to forget that the cross of Christ only has significance as a place where sin is judged for those who have experienced the power of resurrection and the gift of the Spirit of God.

It is true, consciousness of sin can lead to brokenness of spirit and thus to healing and wholeness. But so does the brokenness of spirit resulting from abuse, pain, and suffering! Those who are victims of the abuse of others also need healing for bruised hearts and redemption of a broken spirit. The grace of God avails for all of us as it does for those who are innocent victims of life's injustice and cruelty.

There is no need to make someone whose spirit is broken feel condemned as a condition for receiving grace. In fact, this may well crush the broken spirit and turn what could be a hopeful spiritual experience of recovery of the joy of salvation into a hopeless inward spiral of self-condemnation.

"The Lord is near to the broken hearted," wrote David, "and saves the crushed in Spirit" (Psalm 34:18). God's touch is firm, but light. His Spirit is powerful but not violent. "A bruised reed he will not break, and a dimly burning wick he will not quench" (Isaiah 42:3).

The spiritual goal for the broken spirit is renewal and restoration through the power of God. This is the gift of God, which comes freely to those who receive the Spirit. "For all who are led by the Spirit of God are children of God. . . . When we cry 'Abba! Father!' it is that very Spirit bearing witness with our spirit that we are children of God, . . ." (Ro. 8:14-16).

The effect of suffering, pain, and loss upon the self is a narrowing one. Anxiety causes the self to tighten up. The flow of blood is restricted. Muscular movements become stiff and constricted. The self retreats into isolation and sets up defenses against the intrusion of further pain. The Latin word for anxiety is *angustia*, a word that means narrowness. The first step toward recovery is to overcome the effects of this constriction of the self and to emerge into the larger space of self-expression and relationship with others.

The deep feelings experienced during intense pain and suffering may actually be a narrowing of the flow of emotions by denying the full range of feelings that contribute to the health and creative life of the self.

Growth toward full restoration of creative life builds on the overcoming of the constricting force of anxiety produced by suffering and pain. Overcoming is like crawling out of a raging river that threatens to carry us downstream to our destruction. Having escaped the force of the stream that seeks to pull us under, we have become survivors.

Overcoming in order to be a survivor, however, is not enough. To think of oneself as a survivor may empower the self emotionally and lead to recovery, but it fails to satisfy the deeper yearnings and possibility of the self. Survivors may have conquered an addiction, learned to let go of a tragic loss, escaped from dysfunctional relationships, and been healed of traumatic abuse; but this is still not enough to fulfill the highest potential of the self.

Beyond overcoming is becoming. More than emotional repair is needed. We have not fully recovered until the abundant spiritual life of fellowship with God and relationship with others is restored. Restoration is the fullness of God creating anew a spiritual dimension.

Perhaps we have never experienced this fullness. Or, we have only experienced the longing for it. Each of us has the God-given capacity for becoming what we were created to be. Even our unfulfilled longing is a witness to this capacity. Restoration begins with opening up this capacity and then moving us toward fulfillment. This is the experience of God's gracious Spirit working with our spirit.

It is the spiritual core of the self that gives direction to the emotions and expands the creative capacity of the self. When the irrepressible spirit of creativity, imagination, and vision is unleashed within us, we move away from the security of a fixed center toward the growing edge. It is our spiritual life of faith, hope, and love that enables the self to transcend its narrowness, to move beyond its own history, and create its own story.

Openness to the spirit of others and to supportive relationships is crucial to a process of growth and change. Healing a broken spirit means the recovery of the self in relationship, sustained by a spiritual openness to love, faith, and hope. This is the recovery of the original form of the self as created in the image and likeness of God.

Openness to change is a characteristic of the self that is on the growing edge of life. When brokenness occurs, as it does to all of us, it presents a crisis to the self. Healthy recovery goes through the shock and trauma of pain and loss, but discovers the resources to adjust to the shock and adapt to the change. This is the spiritual aspect of self-recovery, for the self experiences a revitalization of spirit which produces the gift of faith and hope. The reach of the human spirit to the Spirit of God underlies the self's capacity for faith, hope, and, ultimately, trust and acceptance.

With brokenness there is bleeding. Every hurt and each loss is a hemorrhage through which the self bleeds its pain. Left to ourselves, we attempt to staunch the flow as best we can. After a time, the wound seems to be healed, and the pain subsides. Then suddenly, like an aftershock of an earthquake long forgotten, a tremor arises within us, and the hurt spills over again, an embarrassment to us and a discomfort for others.

Healed over pain is like a hidden land mine, one misstep and it blows up right in your face. We should never walk alone in the pathway of recovery. We need companions who have walked that way before and who are safe escorts.

Here we discover the double bind in moving from recovery toward restoration. Without the supportive and affirming experience of others we walk alone like solitary survivors in a crowd. Even so, it is often those whom we trust and those to whom we look for love from whom we receive injury and abuse. Is that not tragic?

Life in relation to others is no protection against abuse, pain, and tragic loss. In fact, shared promises and commitments raise the stakes for our loss and grief. There is something in us that wants to avoid this by withholding commitment and reserving our independence. But solitariness (not solitude!) can be a form of abuse for the human spirit. And walking alone provides no certainty of never falling.

"Two are better than one," wrote the ancient Preacher, "because they have a good reward for their toil. For if they fall, one will lift up the other; but woe to one who is alone and falls and does not have another to help" (Eccl. 4:9-10). There are people who have walked the road to recovery and who have been restored. These are the ones with whom we can find escorts for our own journey.

When we experience brokenness while staying within a community of support and care, there is an interchange, a transfusion, if you please, so that the life that flows out of us flows back into us, filtered through the fabric of intentional care. Within the life of the self in relation to others, there flows the pain of others as well as the joy of others.

Judas could no longer see beyond the consequences of his own act; he had allowed a door to close through which no one could enter, and his perception of reality was as distorted as his own reflection would be in the 'crazy mirrors' at the carnival. The story of Judas is our story, and only when we understand this can the story of Jesus have transforming power in our lives.

Judas now has an escort on his journey. Jesus does not only offer conversation but companionship on the way to healing and hope. The door that Judas closed has yielded to the power of God's grace and love. So too, the power of God's love breaks through our closed doors and disturbs the carefully constructed sequence by which we order our days.

Does Judas see this clearly now? No, not yet. His eyes are still veiled by a film of shame, like the 'shrink wrap' that protects products from direct contact. The veil is lifting though, and a new vision of himself is emerging.

8

Amazing Grace: Seeing Ourselves in the Face of God

There is a child within us, psychology tells us, and that child hides behind the layers of defenses we have carefully built over the years. For many, the child has been abused and feels guilty, as though in being the victim one is also responsible for causing the offense. For some, the child may survive neglect yet continue starving for love and affection. Others nurse the wounds to self-esteem caused by humiliating failure, keeping them under cover, never allowing them to heal. Regardless of the metaphor used, we all feel a private and personal sense of shame when our inner life becomes public knowledge. For we all have been 'caught in the act' at some point in our youthful exploration of forbidden boundaries.

Our very first parents, Adam and Eve, we are told, were bound together in loving intimacy and were both "naked, and were not ashamed." When discovered after stealing the forbidden fruit, they suddenly became aware of their nakedness and "sewed fig leaves together" because they no longer were unashamed. When God approached, they hid themselves from his presence among the trees in the garden (Gen. 2:25; 3:7-8). We are all born as children in hiding, longing to be loved yet fearful of the demands upon the self of the intimacy that love desires. We grow up with veiled faces, as it were, blinded by the shame which exposes us as unhealed.

Jesus does not jump out of the bushes at Judas displaying his resurrection radiance. He approaches with bruises on his wrists and sweat staining his tunic. There is something in the appearance of Jesus that corresponds to the inner torment of Judas. Jesus stands on Judas' side of the veil, for such veils can only be removed from the inside. The resurrected Jesus is still the one who took upon himself the form of the human (Phil. 2:7).

Judas has more than enough reason to feel shame and to dread the approach of Jesus. This dread is as old as Adam and as fresh as our most recent failure. Before Judas can be healed, the veil must be penetrated and the shame removed by liberating the child who hides. Most of us would be clumsy and cruel, but Jesus' touch is the tender touch of healing grace.

VEILS MUST BE REMOVED FROM THE INSIDE

Tell me of the closed doors behind which you crouch and the veil behind which you hide. Are they successful in keeping out the baying hounds that dog your heels? Are the hinges of those doors so well-oiled that they close effortlessly and noiselessly at the first sound of an approaching footstep? Is every conversation a game of opening and closing doors, a ritual that must be practiced daily in order not to fail on Sunday?

Or are there doors which closed so long ago that the final thud still reverberates in the silence? Can we as children close doors that defy our attempts to open as adults? I think so. I have them. I know that they are there. Some of these doors are to keep me out, rather than to close me in. I no longer remember why they were closed, but only that they must not be opened. Behind some doors lie undiscovered and unrevealed shame; behind others the bones of a child, who bears my name, buried in secret in order that the adult should live.

I can live with these closed doors, for I have rooms that are spacious and open outward toward the green prairies and undulating hills. And there are people in this landscape, moving toward me, and I am not afraid. Someday, it would be well for the grace of God to give life to the dreams of this child, to speak the childhood names, to explore with me the other unopened doors, and to dispel unknown fears. There is much to be said for being whole and totally alive.

But I know also that others have only one door to the outside, and that is closed so tightly that no blue sky and fragrant night air can seep in. I heard Judas close that door to his life, and the closing was terrible in its fury and finality. I have listened to the voices behind that closed door, and I heard Jesus talking to Judas. I have no doubt but that it was Jesus, for he was able to go though closed doors after the door of his tomb was opened by an angel and he walked free. And I have told you of what I heard, how Jesus spoke of what really counts and of how even betrayal has its boundary in the forgiveness of the betrayed. This is the power of God's love and grace. We do not merely hang by our intellectual fingernails to the windowsill of heaven in hope of a final solution to death. The living power of God's love stands between us and our worst fears, on our side of the closed doors.

Dare we see the form of God behind our veil? Would we allow that veil to be removed from the inside so that the words of healing, which seem like a mockery to us, might become music to our ears and food for our hungry souls? What if the scales were to fall from our eyes, the veil be lifted, and we were to discover that these human words so tortuously wrung out of our souls are not just a cry for help, but are inspired by the same divine presence who drew near to Judas under the cover of his own darkness?

REMOVING THE VEIL OF OUR
DISTORTED SELF-IMAGE

God's presence is not an image with which we are comfortable. The images that appear on the screen of our perception of life are ones with which we are familiar, while the reality of divine presence seems strange. The stone, sealing the tomb that separated the decomposing body of Lazarus from his grieving relatives, was a perception of reality handed down from generation to generation. When Jesus asked for the stone to be removed so that Lazarus could come forth, his sister Martha protested, "Lord, already there is a stench, for he has been dead four days" (John 11:39). Her perception was of a rotting corpse, while Jesus saw a man dancing in the dark, waiting for the door to life to be re-opened!

Jesus had already questioned the sisters about their belief in the resurrection, and received the answers ordinarily found in theological textbooks. When he claimed, "I am the resurrection and the life," their screen of perception went blank. The immediacy of resurrection power was not familiar to them. They knew how to keep the image of death in focus, but lost the picture when challenged to see life as emerging out of death.

Jesus suggests an "eye operation" (Matt. 7:5) when it comes to seeing clearly our life as God sees it. "Why do you see the speck in your neighbor's eye, but do not notice the log in your own eye? . . . First take the log out of your own eye, and then you will see clearly to take the speck out of your neighbor's eye" (Matthew 7:3-5).

The Apostle Paul changed the metaphor when he wrote of those whose minds were hardened to the good news of God's grace: "Indeed, to this very day, when they hear the reading of the old covenant, that same veil is still there, since only in Christ is it set aside. . . when one turns to the Lord, the veil is removed" (2 Corinthians 3:13-16). It is as though they are kept from seeing the reality of God's presence in Christ through their understanding of the law of Moses as the basis for their relation with God. The irony in Paul's diagnosis is apparent. The very law that was given as a means of understanding the grace of God as liberator and redeemer now had become, as it were, a veil over their eyes concealing that same grace of God in Jesus Christ. The "Lord is the Spirit," wrote Paul, and "where the Spirit of the Lord is there is freedom" (3:16-17).

Shame is more like a veil over our eyes than a speck in our eye. The veil of shame is not opaque--we can see through it, even though it distorts our vision. But we feel that others cannot see us cowering behind the veil. The grace of divine presence not only must come through our closed doors, but also move behind the veil of our shame so as to empower us to remove it from the inside.

We are much like the first disciples. The risen Lord Jesus had to remove carefully the veils over their eyes and enter their space through closed doors in order to shift their perception of reality. We too need our veils removed to experience the risen Christ moving through our closed doors in order to dispel the ghostly images that we have so long taken to be real. Nothing persists so stubbornly as does a false picture of ourselves.

Nothing seems more familiar to us than the view of the world as distorted by a deep sense of self-reproach and shame.

"Some of us are so hooked into shame," wrote Lewis Smedes, "that we are afraid we would be lonely without it. . . If we lost our shame, we would not recognize ourselves."

RECOGNIZING OUR OWN VEILS

We all need our eyes opened to see more clearly the purpose and presence of God's grace in our lives. The veils we wear are various, comfortable, and well-fitting. They should be. We designed them and wear them night and day! But when the veil becomes part of the eye itself, we can no longer, if we ever could, distinguish between the two. I use the metaphor to illustrate that our visualization of life in concepts and images tends to reflect more of what we want to see or are conditioned to see than what is there before us.

Think of how we use the metaphor of sight. Of an incurable idealist or optimist we say that this person sees life 'through rose colored glasses.' Of someone who sees only certain things and misses others we say that such a one has 'tunnel vision.' Of someone who misses the 'big picture' and is overly preoccupied with details we say that he 'cannot see the forest for the trees.' Paul wrote, "now we see in a mirror dimly, but then face to face" (1 Cor. 13:12).

We have each created our own way of seeing; the veil that we wear was created by us. But we cannot remove our own veils. Perhaps, though, we attempt to remove the veil from the eyes of each other too quickly. Do we not often give premature assurance when another is grieving a painful loss? Are not our impatient attempts to strip off the veils of another usually counterproductive and unwise? The therapy of removing veils in order that the eyes of another may be exposed to the vision of God's grace, forgiveness, and love requires human compassion and tenderness accompanied by the Spirit of the risen Christ.

Kierkegaard once told a parable in which a typographical error was given self-consciousness and then told that it would be corrected. The error protested with all of its might, for its only existence was due to an error, and correction meant annihilation. Mental illness is the most stable and resistant to change of all human perceptions. For the very nature of a distortion is to preserve its existence through resistance to change. We tend to think of emotionally disturbed people as unstable and unreliable, when, in fact, such a condition has a stability and predictability that often defies therapeutic intervention. What we mean is that persons whose perception of reality is skewed by distortions of a mental or emotional nature often cannot keep their balance in a world where change, mobility, and creative innovation are required to maintain relationship to reality.

There is a rigidity to distorted perceptions of reality that causes people to snap under the strain of adapting to the unexpected and inexplicable. The suicide of Judas may be such an instance. To end up a failure and a betrayer was so unexpected and so inexplicable that he could not integrate this consequence of his actions into his self perception without breaking under the strain. If Judas is to succeed in removing the veil of shame through the dialogue that we have created, he must have his eyes opened to see more clearly that his act of betrayal was not fatal from Jesus' perspective. He must also undergo a radical shift in his self perception by which he can accept his status as a forgiven betrayer, a child of God, and admit to the grace of God in his life.

CLOTHED WITH GRACE AND
HEALED OF SHAME

We all use coping and defense mechanisms to 'tame the terror of being alive.' None of us could bear to look constantly into the face of total reality, with all of its terror and uncertainty, out what we don't need to know or face in any given moment.

Coupled with this limitation of our perception for the sake of our sanity is the masking of evil as an inner urge and terrible contradiction to our essential goodness as created in the image of God. We would be misled, therefore, to think of distortions in perception as limited to forms of mental illness. There is a theory that some forms of mental illness are due to more penetrating glimpses of reality in its painful and often tragic outlines than 'normal' people permit themselves to see. Too big of a 'dose of reality,' as Ernest Becker once put it, can drive us to become 'normal neurotics' in order to block off what is too painful to see and know.

It is one thing to focus our perception more narrowly in order to create boundaries within which we normally live. This is necessary for our health and happiness, for we are finite beings after all. We need not know all that God knows in order to be human. It is quite another thing to be blind to the evil of which we are capable and so distort our self-perception that we project this evil upon others rather than open it up to be healed by divine love and grace. In some cases, this evil can be concealed in motives and actions that are ostensibly righteous and holy, leading to fanatical zeal against which there is no inner restraint. To have these distorted self-perceptions challenged and revealed is fearfully shattering. But when this takes place in the presence of divine grace and love, our blindness is changed into true vision and doors long closed to communication and communion are opened freely from within.

Through his encounter with the risen Christ in the power of the Holy Spirit, Paul came to view his own life as totally reoriented. As a result, he was able to integrate his former murderous actions against Christians as being actually against Christ, and therefore forgiven and clothed with grace. Openly speaking about his former life of persecuting Christ through these fanatical actions, Paul can say, ". . . though I was formerly a blasphemer, a persecutor, and a man of violence. . . I received mercy because I had acted ignorantly in unbelief, and the grace of our Lord overflowed for me with the faith and love that are in Christ Jesus" (1 Timothy 1:13-15).

Shame is healed, not by exposing failure and weakness, but through empowering the self through the gift of grace and love. Paul not only experienced forgiveness for his sins, but he received the deepest affirmation of self that any person can know, that he was of inestimable value to God! This value was enacted through the choosing of Paul to become a witness to the resurrection of the very Christ whom he had persecuted. Being trusted with bearing the identity of another is the supreme gift to the self.

In the scenario that I have created through the time warp of the resurrection, the dividing line between Judas and Jesus is no longer his suicide, which took place before the resurrection. Jesus has come to give the gift of his own Spirit to Judas and to call him into being a witness to the good news of salvation from sin and death. Judas becomes a child of God, not merely a pardoned sinner!

Would Judas have gone ahead with his self-inflicted death had Jesus actually encountered him as we have imagined it? Not likely. Would the disciples have warmly received Judas back into their midst as they did Peter? We hope so. It would have been difficult for them, but with God all things are possible! Would Judas have been filled with the Spirit at Pentecost along with the others gathered in the upper room? Most certainly.

Would we listen to the Judas who is filled with the Spirit of God as he tells us of his 'gospel,' which he received directly from the Lord, the same gospel as Saul of Tarsus received from the Lord Jesus following his conversion? Absolutely! For in many ways we are each more like Judas than Paul.

"I am the resurrection and the life," says Jesus, "those who believe in me, though they die, will live" (John 11:25). Death has been destroyed. For Judas, as well as for each of us, death no longer has power over us.

Through the power and presence of divine grace, and by the power of the living God, we can come forth out of our tombs, unveiled, as blessed children of God. We would do well to listen to Judas whose heart has been healed and his soul restored. He has good news to share.

Epilogue

The Gospel of Grace According to Judas

I am Judas Iscariot, the betrayer of Jesus of Nazareth. You can call me Judas.

I did not live to experience the resurrection of Jesus, who called me into discipleship and whom I betrayed with a kiss.

I perished from this earth by my own hand, as you have been told. It need not have happened. But that can only be true in retrospect. At the time, the relentless accusations of my heart against myself because of my sin of betrayal became unbearable.

When those who paid me to deliver Jesus to them refused to stop the execution of this innocent man, I thought that I had no place and no one else to whom I could turn. The eleven had already condemned me in their hearts. As they led Jesus away, I even heard one of them say to another, "I knew that he could not be trusted; he was possessed of a demon from the beginning."

I understand why such things are said. The irrational act of betrayal within the bond of love and friendship strikes terror into the hearts of those who witness it. "If this can happen to Judas, how can we be sure of ourselves? Which one of us will be next?" This is why betrayal is so destructive, for it poisons the trust that each one has in oneself and one for the other. The only way to purge this poison, we think, is to give the traitor over to Satan, like a scapegoat, to carry off our own demons.

I cannot blame others for my desperate act, however. The defect was in my own heart, not in their haste to be rid of me. In destroying another's life through betrayal, I felt that I had committed an act for which only my death could atone. It would not save him, of course, but it would put a merciful end to the spiral of accusation, remorse and guilt. I assumed that I alone could pay the penalty for my own act.

I was wrong.

I was a disciple of the Jesus who was crucified but never an apostle of the resurrected Christ. I had no ministry, I am no martyr, and I never became St. Judas! I was once an answer to prayer, but never have I been called to assist in the prayers of others.

THE GOSPEL OF THE BETRAYER

I see that in the canon of Holy Scripture there is no Gospel According to Judas. That is understandable, but for only one reason; I perished from this earth by my own hands before the resurrection of Jesus. That is sufficient reason. Death has a way of silencing one--except for Jesus Christ.

I did not live to write my own story, and those who did remembered me as a traitor. Their story of me is accurate so far as it goes, but incomplete. There were many good days that we shared together during those three years, which they chose not to remember. Who can blame them? I have no need nor desire to complete that account by filling in those days. There is no gospel of the 'good old days'; the gospel has its beginning, as Paul clearly discovered, in Jesus Christ--*descended from Da-*

vid according to the flesh and designated Son of God in power
according to the Spirit of holiness by his resurrection from the
dead, Jesus Christ our Lord (Romans 1:3-4).

No, there is nothing more to be added to the four gospels,
which tell us of the birth, life, death, and resurrection of Jesus
of Nazareth. And there is nothing to be added to the gospel
received by Paul; nothing that is contrary to that gospel can
be accepted as true, even if preached by an angel or an apostle
(Gal. 1:7-9).

What remains to be completed is a story that only I, Judas
Iscariot, can tell. The eleven other disciples, my former companions, each met Jesus after his resurrection and so carried on
the 'tradition of the twelve,' maintaining continuity of witness
to Jesus both before and after his crucifixion and resurrection.
Paul had no part in this tradition but, instead, formed one of his
own, grounded in his own conversion story following the ascen-
sion of Jesus into heaven. There is the 'gospel of the twelve'
and there is the 'gospel of the Damascus Road Conversion,' but
there is not yet a gospel of the betrayer. Between Peter as one of
the twelve and Paul as the 'singular apostle' you will find me,
Judas, both an enigma and a stigma; one who was originally
called as a disciple but also cursed as a traitor. Not merely one
who failed and faltered, only to find healing and hope in Christ,
but one who allowed failure to become fatal, and who drank
the bitter-sweet poison of remorse to the dregs.

There is a story that needs to be told, a gospel that needs to
be preached, to those who live in the space between a robust
Peter and a rambunctious Paul. Those who are never haunted by
the smallest ghost of betrayal and those who are never hounded
by the most relentless demons of remorse and bitter failure may
find Peter and Paul sufficient role models for faith. But for oth-
ers--like me, Judas Iscariot--there is another testimony to Jesus

Christ that can become a gospel of life and hope. The Gospel
of Grace According to Judas is my message to the world. The
heart of the traitor has been healed, the lips of the betrayer have
been unsealed, the voice of one redeemed from self-destruction
is raised in praise of the Lord Jesus Christ.

THE GOSPEL OF GOD'S FORGIVENESS

The most difficult thing for me to forgive in myself was the
fact that I had caused his death upon the cross. But I was wrong!
When he found me in my wretched self-pity and torment, he
clearly revealed to me the fact that his destiny had already been
decided when he came to this earth to take the form of human
life. Under sentence of death, he died to destroy that death and
its power once and for all.

I was slow in grasping this truth, but he was patient and told
me that it had taken him an entire afternoon and a long walk to
Emmaus to convince two others that the Messiah was destined
to suffer and die and be raised again, according to the writings
of the prophets!

Their problem was primarily a conceptual one, a failure to
understand that suffering and death was God's way of taking
sin upon himself.

Mine was infinitely more difficult, for I had personally betrayed the Messiah and contributed directly to his death. My
problem was not merely an intellectual one that could be cleared
up by a new way of thinking. I was morally devastated and psychologically drenched with guilt. No explanation could remove
the guilt I felt for an act of betrayal which led to his death on
the cross. Despair rose up in me like a evening fog, shrouded in
darkness and smothering the last spark of life within me.

Yes, he said, *I know that darkness; it comes with fear. I felt it in my own soul when I prayed in Gethsemane for my Father to remove from me the cup of pain and sorrow. While you were sinking under the waves of your darkness, I was moving into mine. My soul was troubled and I cried out to the Father to save me. But then I understood that it was his purpose and my destiny to die, in order that death may be destroyed once and for all (John 12:27). My sorrow was infinitely greater than that caused by your betrayal. And my pain is healed. I am alive!*

Perhaps it's hard for you to identify with the disciples whom Jesus called. He called so few of us and sent most others back to attend to their business and to live out their lives as mothers and fathers, sisters and brothers, working in the fields, trading in the cities, marrying and giving in marriage, living by the rituals and customs of daily living and dying. This, I know, is what life is like for most of you. Compared to Jesus' particular calling of each of us, you may feel that there is little sense of 'God's calling' in your life.

THE GOSPEL OF GOD'S CALLING

The calling to be children of God's Kingdom was not restricted to the twelve disciples, however. If you read the story of Jesus' teaching carefully, as the others have faithfully told it, you will see that there is a calling of God that every child and each person has. This is a calling to humility as the way to greatness, to a life of service as the way to success (Matt. 18:1-4).

I must confess that I felt this calling as a young child and had visions of fulfilling it in some noble way. Perhaps this is where I began to deceive myself. When Jesus chose me as one of the twelve, I thought that my calling to be a child of God's Kingdom had been confirmed, and I immediately began to think of the sacrificial way in which I could fulfill it--through some extraordinary service perhaps. I even had visions of a glorious victory over the foreigners who occupied our land and saw myself as being called to be in the forefront of the battle, which I was sure would be victorious.

The other eleven survived, despite their own misconceptions, and went on to become apostles of the risen Lord. Their calling may not serve as a model for your own calling from God. My own story is different from theirs. My calling as a disciple was indeed forfeited through my death. But my calling as a child of God's Kingdom was restored and secured through his resurrection! I could not become his apostle, but I could become his friend (John 15:13-14). Jesus did appear to me as the resurrected Lord in the place where I believed there was no forgiveness, and he said to me, *my choosing of you counts more than your betrayal of me*! Through his grace I discovered that the calling of God by which we become children of the Kingdom does not rest upon our faith alone, but upon his faithfulness toward us.

What the ones who hired me to betray Jesus would not hear, God heard. I told them, "I have sinned in betraying innocent blood" (Matt. 27:4). This was not the disciple, Judas, saying this, but Judas Iscariot, the child who once had visions of serving God. No longer just Judas the betrayer, but Judas son of Iscariot, the child of my parent's love, the child whom God had called. Jesus, the risen Savior, assured me that my sorrow had reached the heart of God and that I was heard by him, even though no one on earth could believe me.

My gospel is not that of a successful disciple, one of twelve, but of a child of God who failed and whose failure was not fatal. Yes, it did lead to my death, but this was only because my own heart did not and could not hear the gospel of God's grace and love for me. I am Judas, the child in all of you who at one time had a heart of humility and a dream that was once beautiful and glorious. I have good news. The child that we were created to be is loved by God and can be renewed and restored through Jesus Christ.

It is God's choosing of us to be his children that counts, not our betrayal of that choice. Hidden deeply in our actions of betrayal and faithlessness, is the heart of a child, where a calling to be a child of God can be heard. This capacity cannot be destroyed, either through failure or through self-inflicted death. For death does not have that power; it cannot kill what God has made alive. And what we have killed within ourselves, God can and will make alive through the life of his Son, Jesus Christ.

When I assumed that my failure as a disciple canceled my calling of God, I was wrong. And you are wrong if you feel and think the same way. When I saw that my kiss on the face of Jesus was the last contact I would have with him, and when I knew that this kiss was that of a traitor, I felt that nothing could restore within me the belief I once had in my own capacity to love and trust. But I was wrong. Jesus came back to me after his resurrection and breathed upon me as he did the other disciples, and said, *Peace be with you--receive the Holy Spirit.*

And if you think and feel that your own capacity to love and believe in yourself has been destroyed, this too is wrong. The gospel is not only that Jesus gave his Spirit to those few disciples, or even to those who successfully followed him, but the gospel is that the risen Lord Jesus comes to each person and says, *Peace be with you--receive the Holy Spirit!*

I bruised and broke my own heart because I assumed that failure was fatal. I did not listen to the child within me and hear again the call of God upon my life to seek him in humility and openness of being. I did not wait for his coming to me, but raced ahead to my own destruction, thinking that the only thing that counted was my betrayal.

I tell you that *Jesus is alive and is coming to you*. In him is poured out the depth of divine love and grace, which reaches to the depths of our despair and unbelief and raises us up with him to the heights of joy and peace. I have found peace with God through Jesus Christ, whom I betrayed, but who did not betray me. I have found forgiveness and restoration through the power of his Spirit that flows through me. This is my gospel.

THE GOSPEL OF GOD'S SUFFERING LOVE

It was strange. He did not try to talk me out of my despair and torment; he merely touched it with his own suffering. My sorrow over my own sin had driven me away from God and deep into myself. I had betrayed innocent blood; I had not only abandoned him, I had caused his death. The pain of that reality dripped into my soul as if fed intravenously from a bottle as large as the world itself. No one had suffered in his soul so much as I--of that I was sure.

But I was wrong. He had suffered as much and more, and not because of my betrayal but because of his own death. He had spoken often of his death, but we all appeared not to notice. On one occasion Peter challenged him for that kind of talk and was sharply rebuked by Jesus. Jesus even called him Satan for thinking like that!

Now I understand that the events that led to his crucifixion were complex and many-sided. No single action directly caused this tragedy. But even more important, it was not crucifixion, but dying that removed sin from the world; for death is the consequence of sin, and only when death is destroyed through resurrection is sin removed and its power over us nullified.

It was indeed strange! When I saw him as the innocent Son

of God, it only compounded my own sense of sin and opened a chasm between us. But when he touched my pain with his own, and when he shared with me his own 'loss of innocence' in becoming human under sentence of death, I felt closer to him than at any point in our three years together. I knew then that it was not the love of God from a distance that saves us; through the pain and suffering of a loving God who is with us comes the love that heals and redeems us.

THE STEPS TOWARD HEALING

The inner healing began in my own soul when he touched my anguish with his own godly sorrow. My first step was in being able to share my pain with someone I trusted. And that is strange as well! The very one whom I had betrayed and with whom I had broken trust was now the one person that I trusted! In our own self-inflicted guilt and pain, we trust only another who knows pain. Those who come to us meaning well, but in the superior position of not being guilty themselves, only reinforce the chasm between us. The guilty do not trust the innocent, and the dying do not trust the living. But for trust to begin again, it must be a shared trust issuing out of a shared life. Though he came as the resurrected Lord Jesus, he entered into my pain and loneliness by sharing his own.

The next step in my healing was to move from trust to belief. Could I believe again, first of all in my own words and actions, and then in God's word toward me? It felt good to be accepted for who I was and not for who I was *not*. He approached me as one who had betrayed him, but also as one whom he had chosen and called. My defenses were down and I was stripped of all pretense. As with Adam and Eve, the fig leaves were removed and I stood naked in his presence; yet I was clothed by his love and mercy. I knew that I was guilty; but the shame was taken away, for I couldn't hold on to shame in the presence of such comforting and healing love. I received his forgiveness, and the guilt was removed as though the sword over my head had been removed; and I was free.

I sensed the power of faith rising in me again, as if the childhood dream had not left me after all. I felt that he had infused life into me and brought light into my darkness. But what emerged was my own power of faith and the desire to believe again, to hope again, to *live* again!

Then it was that I felt it possible to love again and to make promises again. Holy Scripture records the dialogue between Jesus and Peter, where Jesus asked Peter three times, "Simon, Son of John, do you love me?" It took three times with Peter-- I won't tell you how many times it took with me! But he persisted, until I could truly say it and understand its implications. Faith, hope, and love grow out of the core of ourselves. When they die, they are born again through the power of the grace of God, whose pain and suffering allow us to trust him, whose belief in us causes us to believe in ourselves, and whose love for us makes us want to love in return.

I was wrong when I assumed that my betrayal had caused his death. I was wrong to inflict upon myself the terrible burden of bearing my own sin and so to destroy myself through guilt. And you would be wrong to feel that the cross of Jesus Christ stands over against you as a sign of his innocence and your guilt. Neither your sins nor mine *caused* him to die on the cross. In allowing himself to be put to death without resistance, he did bear the consequence of our sins. But this he did *because of God's love for us and because of his love and obedience to God, his Father*. We're mistaken when we think that it was our sin, not the love of God that brought Jesus to the point of his own death.

He is never closer to you than in his own suffering and death, because this is what he chose when he became human. Remember who it is that is telling you these things. I am Judas Iscariot, the one who betrayed him, the one who plunged so deep into the pain of remorse, guilt, and despair that only by the grace of God could he be saved. When I approach you, my pain is real, not a therapeutic attitude. My complicity in loneliness and despair is honest, not a pastoral posture. My gospel is trustworthy, for it is the good news of healing and hope, which I myself have experienced and which comes to *all of us* through the risen Lord Jesus.

Come to me, all who labor and are heavy laden, and I will give you rest. Take my yoke upon you, and learn from me; for I am gentle and lowly in heart, and you will find rest for your souls. For my yoke is easy, and my burden is light. I was standing in the very front row when Jesus said these words! I was glad for others who needed to hear them and I watched as many sat down at his feet and let his peace quiet their troubled souls and brighten their faces.

Why did I not remember the words of Jesus when I needed most to hear and believe them? I have tried to tell you, and to warn you as well as encourage you. My assumptions were all wrong, my thinking was twisted, my reasons irrational.

But he found me and with his finger dipped in the darkness of my own despair, wrote on the glass where I expected to see only my own lonely face:

JUDAS COME HOME--ALL IS FORGIVEN!

References

Cover: The cover picture of Jesus and Judas is a still photo from the film *Judas*, produced by Paulist Productions, and distributed by the American Broadcasting Company. The photo is found on the web site: http://www.abc.go.com/movies/judas.html

Title page: The quotation is from Eugene O'Neil, "The Great God Brown," *The Plays of Eugene O'Neil*. New York: Modern Library, 1982, p. 318.

Prologue: The reference to the hound of heaven is from *The Hound of Heaven*, Francis Thompson. New York: The Peter Pauper Press.

Chapter One: The quotation from Anne Morrow Lindbergh is from, *The Unicorn and Other Poems 1935-1955*, New York: Pantheon, 1956, pp. 42-3. The Wiesenthal story is from Lewis Smedes. *Forgive and Forget: Healing the Hurts We Don't Deserve*, Lewis B. Smedes, San Francisco: Harper and Row, 1984, p. 127. The story of Amy Biehl is taken from *The Orange County Register*, Orange County California, July 29, 1998, pp, 1, 16.

Chapter Two: The quotation from Nietzsche is from *Friedrich Nietzsche: Beyond Good and Evil*, Chicago: Henry Regnery Company, 1955, p. 89.

Chapter Five: The quotation from Thomas Wolfe is from *Look Homeward, Angel!*, Charles Scribner's Sons, New York, 1930. The quotation from C. S. Lewis is from *A Grief Observed*. London: Faber and Faber, 1961, p. 57. The quotation from Eugene O'Neil is from "The Great God Brown," *The Plays of Eugene O'Neil*. New York: Modern Library, 1982, p. 318.

Chapter Six: The quotation from Dietrich Bonhoeffer is from Bonhoeffer, *Life Together*. London: SCM Press, 1970, pp. 115-116.

Chapter Eight: The quotation from Lewis Smedes is from *Shame and Grace--Healing the Shame We Don't Deserve*. San Francisco: Harper San Francisco, Zondervan Publishing House, Division of HarperCollins Publishers. 1993, p. 41. The reference to Ernest Becker is from *The Denial of Death*, Macmillan, 1973.

Questions for Individual or Group Reflection

PROLOGUE: JUDAS COME HOME, ALL IS FORGIVEN

Suggested Scripture Reading: Matthew 27:3-5
1. What words come to your mind when you think of Judas?
2. Why do you think that Judas reacted as he did when Jesus approached?
3. What feelings of remorse did Judas express when he realized what he had done?
4. What feelings do you have for Judas after reading their conversation?

CHAPTER ONE: ENCOUNTERING GRACE WHEN WE LEAST EXPECT IT

Suggested Scripture Reading: Matthew 12:31-32 and 26:20-25
1. Is it more difficult for you to forgive a friend who betrays you by revealing a secret than an acquaintance who spreads untrue rumors about you? Why do you think this is so?
2. In what way does an act of betrayal on the part of another cause you anxiety or uncertainty about your own capacity to remain faithful to others?
3. How might these feelings cause you to react toward someone who betrays you or to someone you love?
4. Do you think shame is more difficult to heal than it is to forgive a wrong action? Explain
5. How can forgiveness be expected when the act of betrayal has destroyed the very bond of love and fellowship?
6. Complete this statement: I think that Jesus would have been ready to forgive Judas because . . .

CHAPTER TWO: RECEIVING GRACE WHEN WE LEAST
DESERVE IT

**Suggested Scripture Reading: Psalm 55:12-14 and John
15:12-16**

1. Do you think Judas' failure would have been less significant
   if he had not been one of the chosen twelve? Explain.
2. What strong feelings caused the other disciples to remember
   Judas only as a betrayer and to see him as a scapegoat?
3. Since every member of a community or family based on
   love has the possibility of betrayal, why do we often deal so
   harshly with the one who fails?
4. Each of us needs to have more insight into the family system
   in which we were raised. Thinking back over your own family
   of origin, what were the internal conflicts that allowed some
   to have 'power' over others? Was there someone who thought
   of himself or herself as the black sheep? What can you do
   now to begin to heal some of these relationships?
5. Complete this sentence: I think that love can include the
   possibility of betrayal and can seek the restoration of the
   betrayer because . . . .

CHAPTER THREE: EXPERIENCING GRACE WHEN WE
NEED IT MOST

**Suggested Scripture Reading: Luke 6:12-16; John 16:23-24;
and 2 Corinthians 12:7-9**

1. Why do you think Jesus prayed when he believed that God
   the Father would provide for him in all things anyway?
2. In what ways did Jesus show that he considered Judas an
   answer to prayer?

3. When you pray, how do you respond when answers are not always what you expect?
4. What in your life is like Judas? What does it mean for you to understand that this also is an answer to prayer?

CHAPTER FOUR: SAVING GRACE: BEGINNING THE JOURNEY TOWARD HEALING AND HOPE

Suggested Scripture Reading: Luke 22:31-24 and 1 Timothy 1:12-14
1. What did Judas do that appears to make his actions more serious than Peter's denial of Jesus?
2. Knowing that Jesus would no doubt offer forgiveness if he turned to him, what feelings within Judas can you think of that would have caused him to take his own life?
3. What were the circumstances in your life when you were tempted to think there was no possibility of God's grace saving you after failure?
4. What biblical support can you think of for believing that even our failures cannot cause God to withdraw his grace from us?

CHAPTER FIVE: EMPOWERING GRACE: ENDING THE CYCLE OF SELF-REPROACH

Suggested Scripture Reading: John 10:27-29; 15:16; and Hebrews 2:14-15
1. What experience taught you about relationships that began with promise and trust, but experienced betrayal or failure on either side?
2. What has the Bible taught you about God's faithfulness to his choosing of you when you have failed him?

3. In what ways do you experience a deep assurance of 'being chosen' by God to be his child?
4. What can you say to people who, like Judas, feel that their failures have become fatal?
5. Since the power of death to determine human destiny has been destroyed by the resurrection of Christ from the grave, what assurance and comfort does this give you?

CHAPTER SIX: RENEWING GRACE: AWAKENING THE MEMORY OF LOVE

Suggested Scripture Reading: John 12:27-33 and 1 John 2:1-2

1. What was the 'reason' that Jesus discovered through his prayers for going obediently to his death on the cross?
2. In what sense did Jesus 'deny himself' when he took up his own cross? How does this help you to understand what it means to deny yourself and follow him?
3. Why is it so hard to begin to love again when it is love that has failed?
4. Complete this sentence: When Jesus comes to me as my personal advocate and friend, I know that my sins have really been forgiven and that I am a person of worth because . . . .

CHAPTER SEVEN: TRANSFORMING GRACE: ENVISIONING LIFE IN THE SHADOWS OF DEATH

Suggested Scripture Reading: 1 Corinthians 15:54-57 and Revelation 1:17-18

1. What are the implications of believing that Jesus' resurrection from the dead destroyed the power of Judas's death to determine his fate?

2. Since Jesus has destroyed the power of sin and death, what does this mean for others, like Judas, who have taken their own life?
3. What was the sequence of faith that transformed the fearing disciples into empowered witnesses?
4. In what ways have you allowed the 'logic of sin and death' to destroy your inner sense of peace and well-being?
5. What new insights have you gained that will enable you to experience the liberating power of Christ behind your closed doors?

CHAPTER EIGHT: AMAZING GRACE: SEEING OUR-SELVES IN THE FACE OF GOD

Suggested Scripture Reading: John 20-19-23
1. Why was it so difficult for Judas to respond freely and fully to the resurrected Jesus who comes to offer forgiveness, healing, and restoration?
2. What are the feelings that you would have if Jesus were to encounter you behind some of the doors that you keep closed to others?
3. What are some of the dreams and longings of the 'child within you' that remain unexpressed and unfulfilled.
4. Why does a sense of shame often seem to remain long after we are forgiven for some sin?
5. Can you see the risen Christ as the new boundary of your life? How would you express your affirmation and thanksgiving to God?

EPILOGUE: THE GOSPEL OF GRACE ACCORDING TO
JUDAS

**Suggested Scripture Reading: 1 Corinthians 15:3-10 and
Revelation 1:4-6**
1. How has your perspective of Judas changed?
2. How does your understanding of God's grace as expressed
   through his life, death, and resurrection of Jesus Christ
   grown?
3. Complete this sentence: The 'gospel of grace' has special
   meaning for me because . . . .

Index